GAMES FOR CHANGE GROUP ACTIVITIES

WITH CREATIVE SPIRITUAL CONCEPTS ON THE SIDE

TIM & LISA PROSSER DODDS & FRIENDS

Published by:

Wood 'N' Barnes Publishing & Distribution
2717 NW 50th
Oklahoma City, OK 73112
(405) 942-6812

Cover Art by Blue Designs
Copyediting & Design by Ramona Cunningham
Illustrations by Delores Kroutil of Art House
Photographs by Pam Collins and Brenda Fox

Printed in the United States of America
Oklahoma City, Oklahoma
ISBN # 1-885473-50-8

To order copies of this book, please call:
Jean Barnes Books/Creative Solutions
405-946-0621 • 800-678-0621
www.creativesolutionscatalog.com

DEDICATION

This book is lovingly dedicated to our daughter Bethany.
You bring joy to our hearts and meaning to our lives.
Thank you for teaching us to be parents,
and allowing us to be your friends at the same time.

THANK YOU TO

Kelly Ellison and Harlan Brownlee for their contribution of Contact
Todd Long of Tucker Leadership Lab, Liberty, Missouri
Forefront Youth Ministries, Independence, Missouri
Everett Graffeo for serving as the best spiritual mentor.
The youth and families that have shared their lives with us over the years.

Mony and Dave for their patience and grace
as this project lingered over the past two years.

PUBLISHER'S ACKNOWLEDGMENTS

Wow, what a process! Every book we publish is a great new learning experience, some end up being greater opportunities than others.

Games for Change started out as another one of our fantastic ideas and turned into a project that took us for a two-year, fun-filled ride full of detours and scenic turnouts. But when we arrived at our final destination we knew the trip had been worth all the time and effort.

We started out by adding some creative and fun variations to some tried and true initiatives, threw in a few brand new ideas, and added a twist. We rounded our initiatives out with some spiritual insights for the more open minded groups.

It was our goal from the beginning of this trip to create the kind of book that you could use with your group on the playground, in the business world, or counseling office by day, and then toss it in the back seat only to retrieve it for that evening/youth group for a little spiritual reflection.

We acquired a bus load of traveling companions along the way whose enthusiasm and contributions to the journey made all the difference.

Pam Collins, Kirsten Collins and Dan Hester tried out some of the activities, made suggestions and took some great pictures to deliver the message of the activities.

Kip Pritchard helped get the project off to a promising start by attempting this daunting task at one point and then cheering us on our way.

Chris Cavert and Laurie Frank generously gave both guidance and feedback.

The world's greatest book rebuilding crew ever included: Julie Hines, Lauren Phelps, Jenny Redden, Kacie Roesler-Mize and Michael Wood.

And then the "models" (and their crew) of our fantastic photos: Michelle, Carl & Jacqueline Bell; Travis Cude; Brenda Fox & Lindsey Jones; Callye, Diego, Michael, Rashi, Satchel & Toamey McCollum; Emily Trosper; Brian Wood, the youth group from St. Mark's United Methodist Church of Bethany, OK; the kids from Camp Defy while attending the Ascent Program for Growth Ropes Course, Oklahoma City County Health Department; and the participants in the Freshmen Honor's Program at Oklahoma City University.

Enjoy your journey, and here's your change!!

CONTENTS

Introduction   vii

About this Book   ix

How to Use Games for Change   xi

Presenting and Processing   xii

SECTION ONE: ACTIVITIES   1

20 Things I Love To Do   3

Body Parts   7

Boundaries   12

Cause & Effect   17

Cliques   21

Companions on the Journey   25

Conga Line   29

Cooperative Drawing   32

Cooperative Puzzles   37

Depending on You   41

Face to Face/Back to Back   45

Herding Kittens   48

Holy Mackerel   51

If Ever...   55

Inner Compass   58

Numbermania!   61

Orb-It   65

Passages   68

Peaceable World   72

Santicky, Fanticky, Lim Po Po   75

Shoe Holler   78

Stepping Stones   81

Tin Pan, Bang, Bang!   85

Turning Over A New Leaf   88

You Are on the Other Side   91

SECTION TWO – THE LABYRINTH   95

Problem Solving Walk   101

Affirmation Walk   102

Celebration Dance   102

Letting Go Walk   103

Falling Apart: A Walk for Difficult Times   106

SECTION THREE – CONTACT   107

Appendixes   126

References   131

INTRODUCTION

As veteran youth ministers, we have been playing games with groups for over twenty years. In those twenty years, we have had the opportunity to share with youth in such diverse settings as primitive campgrounds at 7,000 ft. in the Colorado Rockies, in the beauty of a Canadian pine forest, on the beaches of Tahiti and in a quaint village in the middle of Russia. As facilitators, we are always looking for ways to bring meaning to the experience. For us, the meaning often is an expression of our spirituality. In each of those diverse settings one common thread for many youth is the question of how does this experience fit into my developing personal sense of spirit?

This book is a collection of games and activities that we have used to share spiritual concepts with young people. The beauty is that the games can be shared with or without the added dimension of spirituality. If you are working with a group in a faith-based setting, then the spiritual questions may be of value to you in processing the games. The spiritual concepts are meant to be a springboard for discussions, not a complete curriculum. The challenge of working with different groups is that each will process a game or activity differently. Each group brings diversity of thought, opinion, and life experience. Care must be shown to respect these differences.

We believe in celebration of diversity, not merely tolerance. But sometimes tolerance is where we begin. Out of education, we learn tolerance; from tolerance, we learn appreciation and acceptance. When acceptance of diversity is practiced, then **celebration** of diversity is possible.

Games for Change is sure to be a useful tool regardless of your environment. Adventure or Experiential Education is a powerful way to reach young people. We find that games are a great way to share some of life's most important lessons in a way that is open and fun. Enjoy! And please let us know how this book works for you.

Shalom! Lisa and Tim

BEFORE YOU DIVE IN:

The one part of experiential methodology we do not want to leave out is Challenge by Choice, developed by Project Adventure, a leading organization in the field of experiential education. "The concept of Challenge by Choice allows each person to be in control of his/her level of participation. It means that a person may choose what s/he wishes to share with the group about him/herself. It means that a person may choose to be totally involved physically and emotionally in an activity, or choose to sit back and watch. It does not mean that a person sits and reads the newspaper while the group goes about its business. No matter what level of participation an individual chooses, s/he is still part of the group, even if it means being an observer" (Frank, 2000).

WE HAVE COMMITTED THE GOLDEN RULE TO MEMORY;
LET US NOW COMMIT IT TO LIFE.

Edward Markham

About the Book:

SECTION ONE: Contains a collection of 25 activities for groups. We have included some favorite old games with a new twist as well as some original games we hope you enjoy. Each activity includes an introduction, objectives, needs (materials/props/requirements), procedures, processing questions, spiritual insights, going deeper and going wider.

Each activity is appropriate for most any group in most any setting and can stand alone using the objectives and processing questions included. However, you will find that the ⊚ **SPIRITUAL INSIGHTS**, 🐢 **GOING DEEPER** and 🦎 **GOING WIDER** components can be invaluable if you are working with a faith-based organization. These sections emphasize the need for accepting, including, and loving our neighbors, and they provide some interesting, challenging and fun new ways to encourage spiritual growth, tolerance, and understanding.

In compiling this information, it was confirmed to us that the world's religions had many things in common. Below is a list, in alphabetical order, of faith statements from several of the world's different religious communities that, in essence, say exactly the same thing: "Do not hurt others."

Buddhism: Hurt not others with that which pains yourself.
Christianity: Do unto others as you would have them do unto you.
Hinduism: Treat others as you would yourself be treated.
Islam: Do unto all men as you would wish to have done unto you.
Judaism: What you yourself hate, do to no man.
Native American: Live in harmony, for we are all related.
Sacred Earth/New Age: Do as you will, as long as you harm no one.

from Sacred Myths: Stories of World Religions, Marilyn McFarlane

We've added ⌖ **FACILITATOR NOTES**, 🛟 **SAFETY TIPS** and 🌱 **VARIATIONS** where appropriate.

SECTION TWO: Centers on the use of the ⊚ **LABYRINTH**. The labyrinth is an ancient symbol found in many forms on every continent of the world. This section provides group activities utilizing small or large scale labyrinths, hand-held labyrinths, and creating temporary or permanent labyrinths.

SECTION THREE: Focuses on a large group encounter, called 🕺 **CONTACT**. Contact is designed to give large groups a multisensory, kinesthetic experience. Contact incorporates music, movement, trust, and creativity. Each group will bring a new energy and style to their Contact experience. Included you will find facilitation notes and dialogue processing debriefing.

OTHER HELPFUL STUFF:

In the back of this great book we have provided appendixes and references for you to explore.

See Appendix A for the Activity Matrix where you will find a bunch of information at a glance. With one look you can discern the spiritual focus, group size and the amount of room you'll need for the activity to occur. This is all sorted alphabetically by activity, just as they are placed in the book.

See Appendix B for information about webbing circles or Raccoon Circles. Because several activities call for webbing circles tied with water knots, we wanted to make sure you knew what we were talking about. You will find an easy-to-follow diagram along with further explanation in this appendix.

HOW TO USE GAMES FOR CHANGE:

Each activity is broken down into some specifics: Objectives, Needs, Procedure, and Processing Questions.

OBJECTIVES: We have provided some objectives for you here.

NEEDS: This section is where you will find the icons to indicate the suggested group size and the amount of space that would be ideal to work with:

SMALL GROUP   [S] SMALL SPACE

MEDIUM GROUP   [M] MEDIUM SPACE

LARGE GROUP   [L] LARGE SPACE

ANY SIZE GROUP   [GSD] GROUP SIZE DEPENDENT
Any Size

This section also describes the equipment and supplies you will need for each activity. You will be able to find most with ease. A few things might require a trip to the store. Most activities will need little preparation. A few will need a little extra time.

PROCEDURE: This section describes possible ways to implement the activity. If you are a kinesthetic learner, some of the descriptions might be difficult to figure out. In this case, do the best that you can. Once you put some action to the words, you will see what works and what doesn't work. Please, don't hesitate to make the changes you need to better fit your environment. Whatever you do - HAVE FUN WITH IT!

PROCESSING QUESTIONS: We have provided some ideas for you to work with, before, during, and/or after the activity. These questions can help you understand a little bit more about what the activity might bring out in the group. It's also great to come up with your own questions. Using these questions with the activities turns a recreational endeavor into an experiential process, which we want to encourage in the use of this book. This part of experiential education is not easy to implement. We encourage you to read the Presenting and Processing information on pages xiii - xv. In order to more fully understand how to facilitate your group and the results and answers your questions will illicit, you will need to explore other resources on processing.

IF YOU ARE USING THIS BOOK WITH FAITH-BASED ORGANIZATIONS, YOU MAY FIND THE FOLLOWING SECTIONS HELPFUL:

SPIRITUAL INSIGHT: Experiential educators know from experience (pardon the pun) that activities and their processing can expose emotion, insight and real change. So it's not a huge leap to take that energy and discover its spiritual aspects.

GOING DEEPER: You can take these spiritual insights in any direction you would like. Here we've gone a step further and highlighted a relevant belief or tradition from one of many of the world's religions.

 GOING WIDER: But don't stop there, because we didn't. In going wider we took the principle presented in the spiritual insight, dug a little deeper, and discovered some relevant translations of it from other religions.

PRESENTING & PROCESSING

The ultimate goal of an experiential facilitator is to guide participants through their own discovery of new experiences. From these new experiences, participants can learn how to relate new skills, ideas, and behaviors to future life situations.

To do this, it will help to have some knowledge of presenting and processing games and activities. Some established procedures include the "Adventure Wave Plan" outlined in *Islands of Healing* by Schoel, Prouty, & Radcliff (1988) and the *Experiential Learning Cycle* by Nadler & Luckner (1992).

Another common approach to presenting and processing is "Experience...What?," "So What?," and "Now What?" Proper groundwork is important for the "Experience." First you will want to choose an activity that suits the objective of your session. It should be appropriate for the ability and age of the group, and fit within the limitations of your program facilities. Next, you will want to give clear instructions and safety guidelines, then provide ample time for questions before the activity starts. As the group begins, you become the watchful facilitator, keeping the activity safe at all times.

"What?" happens is up to the group. Some facilitators choose to ask questions about what is happening during the activity. Other facilitators wait until the end to ask. Some facilitators ask during and after an activity. This choice is ultimately up to you.

"So what?" were you feeling or experiencing during the activity is next. This is where skills, behaviors, emotions, and feedback are encouraged. Keeping the discussion safe for all individuals will increase the bonding potential of the group and develop the trust levels needed to take future risks.

To complete the cycle, "Now what?" are you going to do with any new information that you have obtained? This stage pushes learning into the next activity and, with hope, into real life situations. Making the learning relevant to future life situations is where behavior change starts.

The hardest part of the experiential process is not giving out solutions to problems. As adults it is easy to tell someone how to do something, especially if we have a solution. However, more knowledge is gained by self-discovery than lecture. Let the group discover what is in the treasure chest. You can provide the key with thoughtful questions.

Preparation, facilitation, and processing are skills enhanced through time. If you are not satisfied with the way you approached a problem, use the situation as a learning "Experience...What" happened? So "What" did you learn from it? "Now What" are you going to do next time? The process is not just for the group. This is what experiential education is all about. There is always something to learn.

I encourage you to obtain more information about the Experiential Process. Several excellent books and training programs are listed in the Reference Section and in the Appendix. A good teacher is also a good learner. Now on to the Adventure!

Borrowed from Games (& other stuff) for Group, Book 1 by Chris Cavert,
© 2 Ed. 1999, Chris Cavert and Wood 'N' Barnes Publishing & Distribution, 800-678-0621.

SAMPLE PROCESSING QUESTIONS

I have included a few questions to help you "get the ball rolling" so to speak. There are also questions included with most of the activities within this book. I have found it difficult to plan the exact questions I will ask during an activity, because I never know what the group will pull from their experience. Generally, I plan a few questions, then adapt to what the group needs at the time.

1. Let's recap what just happened here. What did you see?
2. Who can share something that was helpful during the activity?
3. Who can share something that wasn't helpful?
4. Did everyone express his/her opinion when a choice was available?
5. What effective forms of communication were used in completing this task?
6. What ineffective forms of communication were used in completing this task?
7. How could you improve your own way of communicating?
8. What are some specific examples of when the group cooperated during the activity?
9. How did cooperative behavior lead to the successful completion of the task?
10. What can you do to produce a cooperative environment?
11. What effect did planning have on your activity?
12. How effective was the group at solving problems during the activity?
13. What are the similarities/differences between the ways you have approached solving problems here and the way you approach them at home or at school?
14. What would need to change in order to enhance your problem-solving ability?
15. What were the behaviors that demonstrated leadership?
16. Was it difficult to assume a leadership role in this group? Why?
17. What are the characteristics and qualities of a good leader?
18. What were the behaviors that demonstrated followership?
19. What are the characteristics and qualities of a good follower?
20. Was it difficult to assume the role of a follower in this group? Why?
21. Did you criticize yourself or put yourself down during the activity?
22. What did you say to yourself during the activity?
23. Do you usually get upset when you make a mistake or do not achieve perfection?
24. What could you say to yourself to counteract the put-down messages?
25. What were some ways in which you were successful during the activity?
26. What self-messages did you give yourself when you were successful?
27. Is it hard for you to give someone feedback? Why?
28. Was there a time during the session when you would have liked to give someone feedback but didn't? Would you be willing to give that person feedback now?
29. How did you express appreciation for another person's actions during the session?
30. What are some appreciations that you did not express? Why?

31. How can you improve your skills in giving and receiving feedback?
32. How did this activity make you feel?
33. How did you feel about the activity?
34. What did you find yourself thinking about during the activity?
35. Were there any significant issues during the activity?
36. How were the issues handled?
37. What are some ways the issues could have been dealt with more appropriately?
38. What are some significant differences you have noticed among group members?
39. How did these differences strengthen/hurt the group?
40. What did you learn about yourself?
41. What did you learn about the others in your group?
42. What did this activity remind you of?
43. What did you do today that you were particularly proud of?
44. How can you use what you learned today in other situation?
45. Was your behavior today typical of the way you usually act in a group?
46. Is there anything you would like to say to the group?

Borrowed from Games (& other stuff) for Group, Book 1 by Chris Cavert,
© 2 Ed. 1999, Chris Cavert and Wood 'N' Barnes Publishing & Distribution, 800-678-0621.

FUN HAS A SACRED DIMENSION.

Adriana Diaz

SECTION ONE

ACTIVITIES

20 THINGS I LOVE TO DO!

This activity is adapted from its original version found in James Canfield's book entitled *100 Ways to Enhance Self-Esteem in the Classroom*. Lisa "discovered" it while working with college students back in the eighties. It helps folks begin to look at the influence they have in their own lives. This activity works for groups just getting to know each other or for groups that are established.

OBJECTIVES: Self-discovery and common interests

NEEDS:
• A copy of the handout for each participant
• Pen/pencil

PROCEDURE: Distribute copies of the handout, and give the group four minutes to list 20 things they love to do in the far left column of the page. This will be very easy for some of the group while others will struggle to come up with all 20. It may help if you ask the following questions:

What do you do with your free time?
Where do you spend your free time?
What are your talents or special gifts?
When your mind wanders, where does it go?

At the end of four minutes, or whenever you decide they have had enough time, explain that each of the columns to the right represents a different aspect about what we love to do.

Column 2: Have the group place a "P/A" at the top of the column. In this column they should place a "P" next to the activities they do with other people or an "A" next to those they do alone.

Column 3: Have the group place a "$" at the top of this column. In this column they should place a "$" next to any activity that costs more than five dollars to participate in.

Column 4: Have the group write the word "Mother" at the top of this column. In the column they should place an "X" by those activities they believe would be on their mother's (or mother figure's) list.

Column 5: Have the group write the word "Father" at the top of this column. In the column they should place an "X" by those activities they believe would be on their father's (or father figure's) list.

Column 5: Have the group write the word "Father" at the top of this column. In the column they should place an "X" by those activities they believe would be on their father's (or father figure's) list.

Column 6: Have the group write the word "Peer" at the top of this column. In the column they should place an "X" by those activities they believe would be on their peer's list.

Column 7: Have the group write the word "Date" at the top of this column. In the column they should place the date when they last participated in that particular activity.

Once the last column has been filled out, encourage the group to sit and reflect on what their list of favorite activities tells them about themselves. You might want to write the following questions on the board or have them on the back of the handout.

PROCESSING QUESTIONS:
1. What does your choice of activities tell you about yourself?
2. How does this information make you feel? What surprises you?
3. What values and commitments does your list of "favorite things" express?
4. How do you feel about your list compared to your parent's list.
5. How do you feel about your list compared to your peer's list.
6. What do you need to make more time for in your life?
7. What is keeping you from doing some of the things you love?
8. What things on your list do you do for yourself?
9. What things on your list do you do for others?

You may choose to process this activity in the large group, in small groups or in pairs. This will depend on the trust level of your group and their willingness to open up and share what can be deeply personal about themselves.

 SPIRITUAL INSIGHT: One universal goal is to find balance. Many of us move through life racing to acquire more knowledge, more power, more wealth. Then there are those who become overwhelmed by the difficulties and failures in life and find it difficult not to withdraw completely. We need to find a way to balance isolation and engagement in life. This can only be accomplished by having balance in our spiritual lives.

 GOING DEEPER: Within the Native American tradition is the spiritual symbol of the Medicine Wheel. The Wheel has a number of different uses and meanings, but the central symbol is that of balance. The Wheel takes many forms, but is most often a circle with two intersecting lines. The lines point in the four directions. East is spiritual, South is natural, West is physical and North is mental. The cross at the center of the wheel represents a human being with their arms held out for balance.

The Creator gave every person gifts to help steady us on our earth walk; he gave us skills, talents, desires and needs. The Medicine Wheel is a symbol of that balance from people who sought wisdom and guidance from the natural world.

Questions:
    How does the symbol of balance in life have meaning for you?
    What are some ways you seek to have balance?
    What threatens your spiritual balance?
    What helps you to restore your spiritual balance?
    What symbols have special meaning to you?

 GOING WIDER: In the Going Deeper section, we highlighted a Native American tradition. We encourage you to examine other world religions for their views and practices on balance.

Here are some ideas:

- The Quaker and Shaker faiths have similar roots. They practice a religion that includes a simple, self-sufficient lifestyle. They believe in personal communication with a God who is both male and female and in the ability to find and give voice to the Inner Light. These expressions took the form of hymns and work songs. Have your group reflect on *Simple Gifts* which is the most well known of these.

    'Tis a gift to be simple, 'Tis a gift to be free,
    'Tis a gift to come down where you ought to be,
    And when we find ourselves in the place just right,
    'Twill be in the valley of love and delight.

    When true simplicity is gained
    To bow and to bend we shan't be ashamed,
    To turn, turn will be our delight,
    'Till by turning, turning we come round right.

You might have your group make up a hymn of their own.

- When Muslims make their pilgrimage to the holy city of Mecca, they must leave all luxury and worldly things behind.

    How does simplicity influence balance?
    What are some things you could let go of to bring better balance to your life?
    What do you need to stay in balance?

Twenty Things I Love To Do!

ACTIVITY						
1.						
2.						
3.						
4.						
5.						
6.						
7.						
8.						
9.						
10.						
11.						
12.						
13.						
14.						
15.						
16.						
17.						
18.						
19.						
20.						

BODY PARTS

This is an adaptation of an old icebreaker. It is good for groups that have been together long enough to have an established working culture and climate. Processing this with the large group is important. This can be a time for group concerns to be voiced, so be aware that conflict can emerge. Remember, conflict isn't always negative. Conflict can bring about growth and change.

OBJECTIVES: Teamwork, communication, and appreciating differences.

  NEEDS:
- Symbols of eye, ear, heart, hand, feet and brain (see template)
- Music
- Questions at each station (see template)

PROCEDURE: Divide the number of participants by the number of body part symbols used in this activity. In a large space lay out the six different symbols and the accompanying questions. Explain to the group that when the music starts everyone should dance or move around the space. When the music stops, everyone must place one foot on a body part, with no more than X on each part (X = number of participants divided by the six stations).

When all have landed, have the participants, one at a time answer aloud the two questions on their list. Once everyone has finished, start up the music for another round. No one can stay on the same spot or revisit a spot they have already been on. Groups should not travel together, thus encouraging participants to engage with new people each time. Repeat until everyone has visited all stations.

PROCESSING QUESTIONS:
EYES – What is your vision for this team? What do you see as the strength/weakness of this team?
EARS – Does this team listen to each member? How can the team use ears more effectively?
HANDS – Who are the "worker bees" on this team? Does the team help each other when needed?
HEART – What is at the heart of this team? Is this a caring team?

FEET – Where is this team going? Who are the movers on the team?
BRAIN – Does this team think through decisions? Does this team act with reason?

 SPIRITUAL INSIGHT: Within a spiritual community each person brings a unique set of gifts and talents. While some may be more "up front" talents, everyone's talents should be valued and accepted. The quiet gifts of prayer and service are priceless and to be treasured. Each one should be encouraged to discover their giftedness.

 GOING DEEPER: An Apostle of Jesus named Paul once wrote:

"Now the body is not made up of one part but of many. If the foot should say, 'Because I am not a hand, I do not belong to the body,' it would not for that reason cease to be part of the body. And if the ear should say, 'Because I am not an eye, I do not belong to the body,' it would not for that reason cease to be part of the body. If the whole body were an eye, where would the sense of hearing be? If the whole body were an ear, where would the sense of smell be?

"But in fact, God has arranged the parts in the body, every one of them, just as he wanted them to be. If they were all one part, where would the body be? As it is, there are many parts, but one body. The eye cannot say to the hand, 'I don't need you!' And the head cannot say to the feet, 'I don't need you.'"

Paul wrote again in Ephesians 4:16:

"Under his direction, the whole body is fitted together perfectly. As each part does its own special work, it helps the other parts grow, so that the whole body is healthy and growing and full of love."

Paul talks about the body of Christ and the importance of each different part of the body. He suggests that God has created each member with a reason and a contribution to the whole. No one part of the body is more important than the other. In order for the body to function properly, each part must make its contribution. Paul takes this analogy of the body to represent the community of believers. He suggests that each member of the community also has a part to play, has value and should be honored.

Questions:
How do we honor one another in this community?
Why do some of our gifts and talents receive more attention or recognition than others?
How does feeling jealous of other's gifts or talents impact our community?
What are your gifts in this body? How can you share those gifts?

GOING WIDER: In the Going Deeper section we highlighted a Christian concept. We encourage you to examine other world religions for their views and practices on gifts and service.

Here are some ideas:

- A Muslim leader, El-Hajj Malik El-Shabazz known also as Malcolm X, dedicated his life to uniting all races so that we could live in peace. His journey did not begin with a desire for unity, but rather with a desire for freedom of his fellow African-Americans as a separate nation. On a journey to Mecca, when he saw people with black skin and white skin gathered and worshipping together he felt a great hope, a hope that all races could live in harmony. He realized that happiness and peace could not be achieved alone or as a separate nation. He felt that his vision of hope was a gift from Allah.

   What gifts have you been given?
   How can your gifts contribute to the rest of the world?
   What kind of world do you visualize?

- A quote by Mahatma Ghandi for your group to contemplate and discuss:

   "When a person loses himself into God, he immediately finds himself in the service of all that lives. It becomes his delight and recreation. He is a new person never weary in the service of God's creation."

   How are you serving those around you?
   How does your service to others affect your life?

- Spiritual service must be humble and anonymous love in action. - Anon

   What does this statement mean to you?
   How do you feel you have lived this statement in the world?

BODY PARTS TEMPLATE

The body parts should measure approximately 2 square feet.

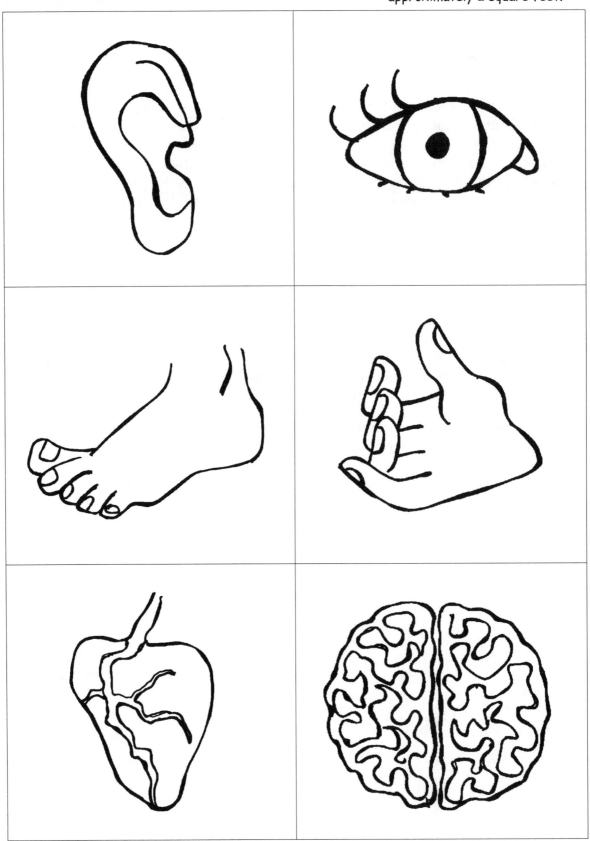

BODY PARTS

EARS
Does this team listen to each member?
How can the team use ears more
effectively?

EYES
What is your vision for this team?
What do you see as the strength/
weakness of this team?

FEET
Where is this team going?
Who are the movers on the team?

HANDS
Who are the "worker bees" on this
team? Does the team help each
other when needed?

HEART
What is at the heart of this team?
Is this a caring team?

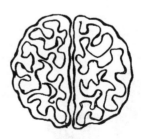

BRAIN
Does this team think through
decisions? Does this team act
with reason?

BOUNDARIES!

This activity is a variation of "The Number Game" by Newstrom, Scannell and McGraw Hill Publishing which can also be found in "Games for Teachers." This is a great activity for those who have difficulty understanding why we need rules. It was first shared with us at a parenting workshop. Over the years, we have seen light bulbs go on over people's heads when they "get it."

OBJECTIVES: Understanding boundaries, guidelines, flexibility, and growth.

NEEDS:
• Two copies of the handout for each participant
• A writing utensil for each participant
• A watch or timer

PROCEDURE: Distribute the first copy of the handout, asking the participants to keep it face down until you say "Start." Explain that on the other side of the handout are the numbers 1 through 64. Their task is to find the number 1, circle it, find the number 2, draw a line to it and circle it and so forth until the time is up or they get to the number 64. Allow them at least 90 seconds. When time is up, ask the group how they did. Did anyone reach 20, 25, 30?

Now distribute the second sheet, asking them once again to keep it face down until you say "Start." When everyone has a copy, ask them to turn over the sheet. This time instruct them to draw a line vertically down the middle of the page and another line horizontally across the middle of the page, creating four quadrants. Then inform them that they will find the number 1 in the top left quadrant and the number 2 in the top right quadrant, the number 3 in the bottom left quadrant and the number 4 in the bottom right quadrant and so on in the same pattern. Quickly begin the second round, giving them the same amount of time as the first round. At the end of the second round, ask them how many improved their score? By how much? Did anyone double their score?

PROCESSING QUESTIONS:
1. Did the first round feel frustrating, overwhelming or exciting?
2. Why did your scores improve on round two?
3. How is this game similar to life?
4. What difference did the guidelines make?
5. How do guidelines/boundaries help us perform better at school, work, home, etc.?

 SPIRITUAL INSIGHT: One of life's challenges is to figure out who we are and what we believe in. Making the time to determine our values and priorities and to discover our talents can help us establish what we want to accomplish with our life. When you take the time to plug in with God and connect with his plan for you, he also connects you with the wisdom and courage you will need to live that life. When your life becomes a true reflection of what you believe, you can make a difference in the lives of the people you love and in the world around you.

 GOING DEEPER: It's important for people around you to know what you're about. What you believe in and what you stand for. It's also essential that they know what brings you down and what you won't tolerate. Where do you draw the lines?

It is important to set healthy boundaries and surround yourself with people who respect them. It is equally important to allow others to do the same. Good boundaries help us maintain the best relationship possible with God, our parents, siblings, friends, acquaintances, teachers and mentors.

To see where you stand boundary-wise, a simple exercise is to place the people in your life within your boundary circle. An example might be:

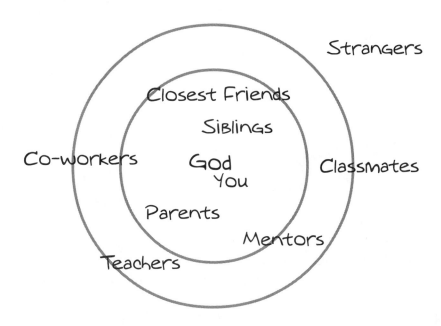

This idea was adapted from *Boundaries: A guide for Teens* by Val Peter & Tom Dowd.

It's also important to remember that boundaries are not walls. They are not made to shut people out of your life, but to protect the choices and beliefs that you have developed to insure good healthy relationships between you and God and others. Good relationships are not always easy, but they are well worth the effort. Following is an empty circle to fill in with your current boundary assessment.

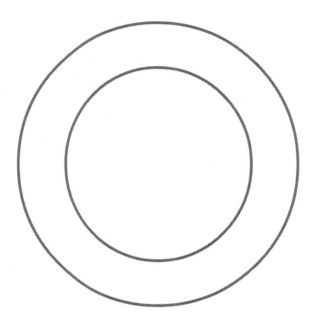

Questions:
How do you feel about the boundaries you presently have set in your life?
What boundaries have you established that you feel good about?
What boundaries do you need to look at again and possibly re-adjust?
Do your family and friends respect your boundaries?
What do you want to accomplish with the boundaries in your life?
Do you respect the boundaries of others?

GOING WIDER: In the Going Deeper section we highlighted the subject of boundaries. We encourage you to examine other world religions for their views and practices on defining beliefs and boundaries.

Here are some ideas:

- Matthew, one of Jesus' disciples tells the story of Jesus entering the temple and driving out the merchants and their customers. He knocked over the tables of the money changers and the stalls of those selling doves. He said, "Scriptures declare, 'My temple will be called a place of prayer,' but you have turned it into a den of

thieves!" The blind and the lame came to him, and he healed them there in the
Temple.   Matthew 21:12-14

   How does Jesus' example in this situation impact you?
   Have you had to make a stand for what you believe in?
   Would you share what that was like?

• Thich Nhat Hanh [pronounced "teek naught hawn"] is a Buddhist monk. In the
  1960's he was a highly respected writer and teacher in Vietnam. When conflict
  broke out, he tried to persuade the leaders of the world not to go to war. He
  published a peace magazine and marched in nonviolent protests against the war.
  This was considered an act of civil disobedience. Because of his beliefs against
  violence and his active stand against the war, he was exiled from his country and
  has never been allowed to return. This has not stopped him from spreading his
  message of love, nonviolence, and mindfulness and continuing his mission for peace.

  Presently, Thich Nhat Hanh teaches at Plum Village, a retreat center in France. He
  welcomes visitors of all faiths, and he shares with them his belief in the power of
  simple actions, such as meditation and peaceful protest, to heal the world.

   How does Thich Nhat Hanh's example in this situation impact you?
   Have you had to make a stand for what you believe in?
   Would you share what that was like?

BOUNDARIES HANDOUT

Cause & Effect

This activity is a great way for your group to see how every action has a reaction. We suggest starting out on a humorous note and moving into more serious topics depending upon the development and maturity of your group. Lisa once facilitated this with 90 sixth graders at once. It was amazing to see the creativity and ability to tackle some serious issues in a fun way.

Objectives: Listening skills, creativity, and understanding cause and effect

Needs:
- 3" x 5" cards with the following statements (see template):
  1. My shirt has a hole in it.
  2. My shirt has a hole in it because a hawk landed on my shoulder.
  3. A hawk landed on my shoulder because I was standing in a field.
  4. I was standing in a field because my dogs ran away.

Procedure: Gather the group into a circle. Ask for four volunteers to introduce the game. Without any front loading (instructions leading into the game), hand the four volunteers the index cards and ask them to read their statements in numerical order.

Once all four statements have been read, ask them to repeat the sequence. Then ask one of the four to add to the story in the same manner as the sequence.

If the fifth statement is done correctly, the phrase "my dogs ran away because..." should be repeated and then another phrase added to finish the statement. Then point to another in the group of four and continue until each has created a new statement. (If the fifth statement is not stated correctly, ask another person in the group to try to follow the sequence.)

Once the group has completed the additional statements, talk to the larger group about the relationship between cause and effect. Discuss how every action has a reaction. Like a pebble being thrown into still water, the ripples are the reaction to the action.

Ask four new volunteers to begin a new series. Here are some starting suggestions:
- My shoes fell off the top of the car.
- There is a hole in the tent.
- The baby is crying.
- The room full of people fell silent.
- Our group leader is proud.

PROCESSING QUESTIONS:
1. Tell about a time when your actions caused reactions. What was that like?
2. Did you enjoy the challenge of creating a reaction in the story?
3. What's the difference between reacting and responding?
4. What did you find most challenging in this game?
5. How does listening impact this game?

 SPIRITUAL INSIGHT: Our spiritual lives are impacted by the choices we make every moment of every day. Sometimes we move through life without a plan or clear direction. We drift from choice to choice.

> What would be the result of becoming intentional in our choice to seek God every day?
>
> How would choosing to seek truth, knowledge and the divine in our daily life impact our other life choices? How would it change us? How would it change our priorities?
>
> What does intentional spiritual growth look like?

 GOING DEEPER: The following is an adapted informal Jewish prayer that is said before studying the Torah.

> "I seek truth from the depth of my being. I do not want to be limited by my own narrow-minded conception of what it should look like. I will open myself to this journey of learning with one condition: Whatever is true should enter my life and take root. Whatever is false should pass through and leave no impression. I trust that it will be so. I embrace truth and deflect falsehood."

In its original form, the prayer is addressed to the Divine Source of all knowledge. Deep within the Judaic faith is the search for truth and knowledge. Judaism has a rich tradition of being intentional in study. The prayer above is meant to enhance the learning and direct it to a particular end. The prayer expresses what you hope to accomplish through your search and empowers that desire.

> Questions:
> How are you being intentional in your search for truth and knowledge?
> Does being intentional in your journey seem comfortable or awkward?
> How do you determine what is truth and what is not?
> How do the choices you make in life affect your spiritual growth?
> How can this kind of prayer enhance your study of the divine?

 GOING WIDER: In the Going Deeper section we highlighted a Jewish tradition. We encourage you to examine other world religions for their views and practices on choice and accountability.

Here are some ideas:

- Destiny, Karma, predestination, fate, kismet - all of these words designate the future as something that has a design. The fact that we humans don't know that design is not a hindrance, it is a blessing. To let go and not worry about what will happen is to grab hold of freedom.

  Transcendental philosopher, Ralph Waldo Emerson, said destiny is "whatever limits us."

  The mystical text, *The Cloud of Unknowing* by St. John of the Cross, states, "We must forget what we believe we know is true in order to really know."

  > How does this information affect your decision making process?
  > How are knowledge and accountability linked?
  > How do you make choices? What do you consider?
  > Share your own beliefs about choice and accountability.

- John Lennon's song "God," lists the things he no longer believes in. Things that actually limited his beliefs. "I don't believe in magic, I-Ching, Bible, tarot, Hitler, Jesus, Kennedy, Buddha, mantra, Gita, Yoga, Kings, Elvis, Zimmerman..." He even names the Beatles as a belief that limited him.

  Make your own personal list of past beliefs that you no longer make a part of your life. "I don't believe in..." Try to list the really intimate and self-defeating ones. End your list by naming what you do believe in.

  > This idea is taken from *Shaving the Inside of Your Skull* by Mel Ash

CAUSE & EFFECT QUESTIONS

2. My shirt has a hole in it because a hawk landed on my shoulder.

4. I was standing in a field because my dogs ran away.

1. My shirt has a hole in it.

3. A hawk landed on my shoulder because I was standing in a field.

CLIQUES

This one comes from *Games (and Other Stuff) for Teachers* by Chris Cavert and Laurie Frank. It is a classic for getting participants to let down their barriers to others in the group.

OBJECTIVES: Problem solving, sharing, inclusion, helping, trust, and verbal communication.

NEEDS:
- A few rolls of masking tape (rope can also be used). It would be ideal if every group of three could have their own roll, but groups can share (a nice social skill).
- The following list of questions to generate some verbal communication:

Are you more like..

a flower or a weed?	a follower or a leader?
endless or fixed?	half empty or half full?
an inhale or exhale?	morning, noon or night?
black or white?	a listener or a talker?
a mast or a rudder?	a "why" or "why not?"
a fountain or a waterfall?	infinite or limited?
sunshine or moonlight?	family or company?
the desert or the forest?	the puzzle or the solution?
a bird's song or a frog's croak?	the sunrise or the sunset?
a giver or receiver?	a hand or a foot?
rain water or well water?	lost or found?
a sun lover or a stargazer?	horizontal or vertical?

(borrowed from *Are You More Like...?: 1001 Colorful Quandries for Quality Conversations* by Chris Cavert & Susana Acosta)

PROCEDURE: Clear the game area as much as you can. Ask participants to get into groups of four. More than likely they will get together with the participants they are comfortable with--cliques of a sort. Using masking tape or rope, ask each group to create a box or other shape on the floor big enough for all their group members to fit into with just enough extra room for a small trash can. (No, you don't need a trash can. We just wanted to state in simple terms that the squares should not be too big.)

Ask all the players to put both feet inside their square. Have them introduce themselves to everyone else in the square (another good social skill). Then use one of the questions provided to initiate some verbal communication within the clique. Ask for their attention and tell them that when you say "change," each player must move to another square. When all players have both feet inside a new square, ask them to introduce themselves to all the people in that square. Then ask another question. Do this mingle/change for a few rounds. Observe the interaction.

Then before each change, start taking away one square at a time by pulling up the tape or removing the rope. Obviously there will start to be more people in each square. Don't forget the introductions and intriguing questions.

 SAFETY TIP: As the rounds progress, you will want to be very safety conscious. Students will start to "hang" off each other. Do not let the students piggyback (hard to have both feet in a square this way, too). Try to suggest some helpful ways to stay in the squares. I also tend to remove the squares near desks and other objects that participants might fall onto. Or, you might use the desks or tables to your advantage so participants can hold themselves up – using the resources around them. When it comes down to a couple of squares, make sure these are in the middle of the room. Depending on the size of your group, you might not want to go down to one square. The key is to create a challenge for them. They will have to find a way for all the participants to have both feet in a square.

The most common solution is sitting down on the floor and resting their feet inside the box instead of struggling for balance while trying to stand.

This is a challenging problem to solve. If you do this activity early on, the objectives are more toward verbal communication, sharing and helping – with maybe a little problem solving. End the activity when the groups have had a little challenge and are still able to fit in the squares with some physical help – getting down to maybe three or four squares. Use the "get acquainted" questions and end with success. If this is a longer standing group or more developed in their challenge-solving skills, try to get down to one square. All of this will depend on the maturity of your group and how far you want to take them.

PROCESSING QUESTIONS:
1. Think about the first group you were in. Why did you choose this group?
2. What was comfortable about this group?
3. When you changed "squares," did you stay with the same group or get in a "square" with new people?
4. Did you talk to someone that you normally wouldn't talk with?
5. What was your reaction to the "squares" being removed?
6. How many feet did you get into one "square"?

 SPIRITUAL INSIGHT: It is harder to have compassion for someone we don't know. Yet, in our self-contained world, we often isolate ourselves from others, only letting in those we already know. Living this way holds us back from experiencing the richness of people who may not be "like" us. The human fabric is a tapestry of many different textures, colors, and styles. The beauty lies in our differences. The challenge is to step out of our comfort zone and experience the beauty of our human family.

 GOING DEEPER: Hinduism is the largest pluralistic religion in the world. Pluralism teaches that there are many paths, many sages, and many holy books and that no religion can claim any exclusive or final representation of truth. On the contrary, Hinduism recognizes a total and profound unity, a unity that is broad enough to allow for diversity.

This Hindu pluralism has confused people coming from "one truth" religious traditions, such as those dominating the Western world. It has caused them to look upon Hinduism as a collection of cults or sects rather than a consistent religious heritage. However, Hinduism has much wisdom to teach everyone. Today in our emerging global society, we must learn to handle the great diversity of human beings and their often very different cultures. Hinduism is built upon diversity and holds within itself an amazing, even bewildering, variety of teachers and teachings. Hinduism seeks to preserve and celebrate diversity.

Questions:
How would having many different beliefs and/or truths challenge you?
How do religious differences separate us?
What is difficult about accepting someone whose beliefs are very different from our own?
Do you agree with the term "religious tolerance"? Why or why not?
Have you ever studied religions other than your own?

 GOING WIDER: In the Going Deeper section we highlighted an aspect of the Hindu religion. We encourage you to examine other world religions for their views and practices on appreciating diversity.

Here are some ideas:

- An apostle of Jesus named Paul once wrote "In Christ there is neither Jew nor Gentile, slave nor free, male nor female; for you are all one in Christ Jesus." In this scripture, Paul tells us that Jesus lived a life in which he treated everyone he met with love and respect and that it did not matter which groups they belonged to. Paul suggests that within a Christian community we should be accepting, embrace diversity, and live together as one.

  How does prejudice keep us from being one?
  What does "one in Christ" look like?
  Have you ever experienced a true community? What was it like?
  How can this group create community?
  Why is it important to have diversity in community?

- Have the group reflect on this Sufi teaching story:

  "Some Indians kept an elephant in a dark room. Because it was impossible to see the elephant, those that wanted to know something about this exotic beast had to feel it with their hands. The first person went into the darkness and felt the elephant's trunk and announced, 'This creature is like a water pipe.' The next person felt the elephant's ear and asserted, 'No, it's like a giant fan.' A third person felt the elephant's leg and declared, 'That's not true. This animal resembles a pillar.' A fourth person felt the elephant's back and concluded, 'Not at all. It's like a throne.' Different points of view produce different opinions. If someone had brought in a candle, they would have all felt like fools."

- Another quote for reflection comes from the Hindu sage Mahatma Ghandi:

  "Religions are different roads converging on the same point. What does it matter that we take different roads so long as we reach the same goal? I believe that all religions of the world are true more or less. I say 'more or less' because I believe that everything the human hand touches, by reason of the very fact that human beings are imperfect, becomes imperfect."

  Do you agree with this quote? Why? Why not?

COMPANIONS ON THE JOURNEY

This is one of our favorite closing activities when a group has been working together and they are ready to depart and go back to the "real world." It is also one we have used at the beginning of a camp, for the staff to be unified and ready to serve together for the week. It does take some up front planning, but the results are worth the effort.

OBJECTIVES: Community building, being prepared, and developing strengths.

NEEDS:
- A 10" square of fabric for each participant
- A ribbon or cord 14" long for each participant
- A teaspoon of each of the following herbs for each participant: sage, lavender, mint, mustard, basil, oregano, thyme, rosemary, dill, cinnamon, orange rind

PROCEDURE: Bring your group together in a circle, on the ground or at tables. Each person will need a flat space in front of them to create their pouch. Begin the activity by talking about a Native American custom of creating a journey pouch. In some Native American tribes, when a warrior or other person leaves on a journey, it is not uncommon for them to take small symbols of their home or family with them, along with herbs or plants that symbolized strengths they might need on their journey.

Distribute the fabric squares and cording materials for making their individual containers. Then begin to introduce each herb by telling the group what it is and what it symbolizes (see the list below). Pass the herbs around the circle and encourage the group to smell and feel the distinct qualities of each herb. Invite each participant to take a small amount of each herb that they believe symbolizes an attitude/quality they have or need for their journey.

FACILITATOR NOTE: A good, inexpensive source for the herbs and plants is your local gardening store.

The following is a list of herbs and their characteristics:

Sage	Courage	or	Self Control
Lavender	Tenderness	or	Hope
Mint	Humor	or	Peace
Mustard	Tenacity	or	Faith
Basil	Flexibility	or	Gentleness
Oregano	Originality	or	Strength
Thyme	Persistence	or	Humility

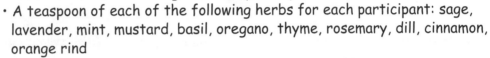

Rosemary	Love	or	Acceptance
Dill	Honesty	or	Patience
Cinnamon	Heritage	or	Grace
Orange Rind	Creativity	or	Kindness

You may want to share this traditional Navajo Prayer with the group:

As I walk, as I walk
The universe is walking with me
In beauty it walks before me
In beauty it walks behind me
In beauty it walks below me
In beauty it walks above me
Beauty is on every side
As I walk, I walk with Beauty.

 VARIATION: Invite the group to make any type of container (using clay, metal, wood, straw, etc.) to hold their symbols/tokens for the journey. Have the group find physical symbols/tokens (a stone, a piece of bark, a paper clip) from their surroundings to include in their pouch and/or have them bring tokens with them. Have the group members introduce their tokens by telling the group what each one is and what it symbolizes.

PROCESSING QUESTIONS:
- What did you think about while you prepared your pouch/container for the journey?
- What do the herbs/tokens you picked symbolize to you?
- How does having a pouch full of things of your choosing make you feel?
- Do you feel that you have all that you need?
- Is this something you would be willing to give to someone else?
- Are you pleased with what you have made?

 SPIRITUAL INSIGHT: On the journey of life, we have many paths to choose from. Each path, however, holds challenges, trials and sometimes difficult realities. Knowing that life is not always easy or fair can help us ask for God's blessing along the way. God desires to bless us even before we know to ask. Asking God to fill our life with the gifts and blessings we need for our journey enables him to give us what he knows we will need to face the difficulties on the journey.

 GOING DEEPER: Within the Jewish faith, Sukkoth or Sukkot (celebrated the fifth day after Yom Kippur - in the fall) is a holiday rich in tradition and meaning. Named after a temporary dwelling, Sukkoth is a week-long holiday focused on celebrating God's relationship with the Jewish people when they were freed from slavery in Egypt.

Sukkoth commemorates how protective "Clouds of Glory" surrounded the Jewish people after they left Egypt and during their forty years of wandering in the desert. It also commemorates how the Jews lived in temporary dwellings during that same time.

> "In Sukkoth you shall dwell seven days, every citizen in Israel they shall dwell in Sukkoths, in order that your generations shall know, that in Sukkoth did I cause the children of Israel to dwell, when I brought them forth from the land of Egypt."
>
> Leviticus 23

The central theme of this season is the pure joy of having a relationship with the Creator and the blessings provided by him. Being surrounded by the walls of the temporary hut is a symbol of how we are surrounded by the constant, protective presence of God himself.

Questions:
   When/How have you felt the presence of God in your journey?
   How have you been blessed by God in your life?
   In what ways do you celebrate God's blessings in your life?
   What struggles have you faced in your journey?
   Is God still present when we struggle?
   What are you in need of right now on your life journey?

 GOING WIDER: In the Going Deeper section we highlighted a Jewish tradition. We encourage you to examine other world religions for their views and practices on blessings for the journey, faith and trust.

Here are some ideas:

• Pilgrimage is a common tradition in most religions of the world.

   • Christians travel to the Holy Lands and to the shrines and birth places of the saints.
   • Hindus have many sacred destinations, including the Ganges River.
   • Buddhists travel to places that relate to Buddha's life.
   • Muslims travel to Mecca to fulfill the fifth pillar of the Islamic faith.

There are numerous other traditional pilgrimages made in the name of religions in the past and today. No matter where the sacred site is or how far the pilgrim travels, there is a point uniting all of these journeys. They are a physical ways of traveling down the inner path to oneness, enlightenment and peace. The pilgrimage is another tool used by those seeking a closer connection to their God.

   What pilgrimages have you taken?
   What pilgrimages would you like to take?
   What sort of journey are you on at the moment?

(The labyrinth was developed as a substitute for those who could not make the physical journeys. See Section Three on the Labyrinth.)

- A quote for reflection from Henri J.M. Nouwen's book entitled *Bread for the Journey*:

  "This is what life is about. It is being sent on a trip by a loving God, who is waiting at home for our return and is eager to watch the slides we took and hear about the friends we made. When we travel with the eyes and ears of the God who sent us, we will see wonderful sights, hear wonderful sounds, meet wonderful people...and be happy to return home."

  How would you describe your present journey?
  What part does God play in your journey?
  How does this quote change your perspective?

CONGA LINE

This activity is from our lively and gregarious friends from the UK, John Bergman & Saul Hewish. In fact we borrowed it from their book of role plays entitled *Challenging Experience*. This activity is sure to prompt the group to explore their view of dependence, become more sensitive to thoughts and feelings, and last but not least it's a goodie for fostering group trust.

  OBJECTIVES: Trust, sensitivity, and dependence

PROCEDURE: Have the group line up one person behind the other. Everyone except the person at the front of the line should put their hands on the shoulders of the person in front of them and close their eyes. The person at the front of the line then begins to move slowly around the area. Have them stay connected to the person in front of them as they move. As the group gains confidence, ask the person at the front to vary the height and direction as they move. Then, throw in some fun, challenging movements.

 SAFETY: One facilitator should mind the back of the line as the tail end can "whip" if the group is traveling too fast. Group leaders should ensure people are safe and that they have their eyes closed.

PROCESSING QUESTIONS:
1. What did it feel like to move with your eyes closed?
2. What did you have to do to stay connected?
3. What did you have to do in order to avoid opening your eyes?
4. What did this exercise remind you of?
5. What did it feel like to lead the line?

 VARIATIONS:
Have everyone line up just as before, but this time have them leave their eyes open. And rather than touching the shoulders of the person in front, they must stretch both of their hands out to about 6" away from the shoulders.

The line should carefully start to move forward like a train. At a signal from the group leader, the train should suddenly stop. Check to make sure people are not bumping into each other.

PROCESSING QUESTION FOR VARIATION:
1. How does this exercise differ from the first?
2. How did you focus on not bumping into each other?

 SPIRITUAL INSIGHT: Working on personal growth and spiritual growth issues can be a very satisfying life goal. Many times we are stunted in our growth because we are unwilling to seek help. To become fully alive and aware, it is important to look for and accept those in our life who can serve as guides. Many mentors or guides are available to you at different times of your life. They have been where you are now and can help you through whatever you currently face. Remember that we are all here to share the journey and sometimes we are the guide and other times we are the guided.

 GOING DEEPER: Within the Jewish faith are special spiritual guides. The spiritual leader of the community is called a rabbi. Rabbi literally means "teacher," but their role goes way beyond that of teacher. Some would say they are a lawyer, teacher, social worker, pastor, and friend all rolled into one.

The full requirements for a rabbi are explained by Maimonides (Mishneh Torah, Laws of Sanhedrin 2:1,7):

> "Only wise and understanding people are to be appointed to the Sanhedrin. They must be experts in Torah law, with a wide breadth of knowledge. They must also know secular subjects like medicine, mathematics, astrology and astronomy."

A rabbi must possess at least these seven qualities: Wisdom. Humility. Fear of God. Aversion to materialism. Love of truth. Pleasant and likeable. An unimpeachable reputation. Rabbis are called upon to be a guide to many on their spiritual journey.

Questions:
Have you had a special guide or mentor on your spiritual journey? Tell us about them.
What are some qualities you might look for in a mentor?
Have you ever been a guide for someone else? How did that feel?
Why is it important to reach out to others for guidelines?

GOING **W**IDER: In the Going Deeper section, we highlighted Jewish tradition. We encourage you to examine other world religions for their views and practices on mentoring and guidance.

Here are some ideas:

- Mentors are found in most religious traditions:
    - A Hindu mentor is called a Guru, which means "he who guides you from darkness to light."
    - In Africa, religious teaching and traditions are handed down orally from the Elders who hold that knowledge and are looked to as guides and as the keepers of truth.
    - In ancient Greece, Socrates, the first of the Greek philosophers established a type of mentoring that is referred to today as "Socratic." Socrates would work with his students, analyzing and examining an idea from all possible angles in the pursuit of truth.

    Who do you believe would be a good mentor to you?
    Name someone who is no longer living that you would have chosen as a mentor?
    Why is it important to seek out mentors in your life?
    What qualities do you look for in a mentor? Do you have those qualities in your life?

COOPERATIVE DRAWING

This activity comes from the curriculum of the Children's Peace Pavilion, a museum designed to teach children how to be peacemakers. It is very effective with youth and adults as well. The key is to make sure the communicator does not try to control the artist, but to guide the artist. There is a big difference!

OBJECTIVES: Cooperation, communication, teamwork, and understanding physical challenge.

 NEEDS:
ANY SIZE GSD
- Blindfolds
- Markers
- 11" x 14" paper
- 2" x 20" strips of fabric or some bandanas
- 3" x 5" cards with the drawing assignment on them (see template)

PROCEDURE: Have the group divide into teams of two. Explain that they will be creating a drawing together. Have them choose who will be the blindfolded artist and who will be the communicator. Next, the teams must tie their wrists and elbows together with the fabric strips or bandanas.

FACILITATOR NOTE: The artist's writing hand should be tied to the communicator's hand. Wrists should be bound so that the hands are facing away from each other. Although they will be using the hands that are tied together to draw with, the communicator should not try to control the hand of the artist.

Have the communicator pick an assignment card and communicate to the artist how to draw the assignment. At no time can the communicator say what the drawing is – only where to place the marker and how to draw. Once the drawing is complete, have the artist guess what s/he has drawn before taking off the blindfold.

PROCESSING QUESTIONS:
1. How did it feel to be blindfolded.
2. How did it feel to be the communicator?
3. Did you succeed as a team?
4. How do you define success?
5. Was it difficult? If so, why?

6. Have you experienced physical limitations in life?
7. Tell about a time when you assisted someone with physical limitations.

 SPIRITUAL INSIGHT: For many people the idea of being "out of control" is very frightening. They put tremendous amounts of time and energy into trying to control the world around them. However, if they take a good look at the world they live in, they will see that many aspects of life are not within their control. Accidents happen, people behave in ways that are illogical, nature is unpredictable. If you are spending time and energy trying to "control" your world, ask what it is that you might be afraid of. Letting go of unrealistic fears can free you to enjoy a world of wonder, mystery, and surprise.

 GOING DEEPER: Lao Tzu, a Chinese philosopher and the father of Taoism, was a wise and learned sage. He compiled eighty-one writings that are called *Tao Te Ching*. One of the central concepts of Tao is wu-wei. Wu-wei is the belief that by "doing nothing" one can "accomplish everything." Within the philosophy of Taoism, Lao Tzu writes:

"Empty yourself of everything.
Let the mind become still.
The ten thousand things rise and fall while the Self watches their return.
They grow and flourish and then return to the source.
Returning to the source is stillness, which is the way of nature.
The way of nature is unchanging.
Knowing constancy is insight.
Not knowing constancy leads to disaster.
Knowing constancy, the mind is open.
With an open mind, you will be openhearted.
Being openhearted, you will act royally.
Being royal, you will attain the divine.
Being divine, you will be at one with the Tao.
Being at one with the Tao is eternal.
And though the body dies, the Tao will never pass away."

In North American culture, there is seldom time for stillness. Yet for over two thousand years the concept of meditation and spiritual centering has been practiced by many eastern philosophies. Within Taoism, accepting the natural flow of the universe and accepting the circumstances of life creates a sense of stillness within the soul. As stated in this writing, stillness will lead to an open mind, an open heart and being at one with the Tao.

Questions:
When do you feel the need to seek stillness?
What gets in the way of creating stillness in your life?
What do we really control in life?

How could accepting the natural flow of the universe be freeing to you?
Does the concept of "do nothing" appeal to you or confuse you? Explain.

 GOING WIDER: In the Going Deeper section, we highlighted a concept from the Taoist tradition. We encourage you to examine other world religions for their views and practices on letting go and open-mindedness.

Here are some ideas:

When we let go of fear, when we find stillness in our lives, when we open our hearts and minds, we are opening to infinite possibilities. We are given the opportunity to achieve our goals and dreams.

• Have the group reflect on Isaiah 43:2-3:

> "...Don't be afraid, for I have ransomed you. I have called you by name; you are mine. When you go through deep waters and great trouble, I will be with you. When you go through rivers of difficulty, you will not drown! When you walk through the fire of oppression, you will not be burned up; the flames will not consume you. For I am the Lord, your God, the Holy One of Israel, your Savior."

    What are some of the fears you live with?
    How does this scripture change your perspective?
    How does this promise make you feel?
    How could believing this promise change your life?

• The Hindus have a meditation practice, "Neti, Neti" or "Not here, not here," meaning that God is not here. Have your group spend several minutes looking closely at the things around them and saying to themselves, "Not here." Then have them point to their heart and say, "Here, here." This is a good exercise to repeat when you become obsessed with or distracted by something.

    How does this mediation practice change your perspective?
    How does this exercise make you feel?
    Is this a practice you want to make a part of your life? Why or why not?

Now, ask the group to look around and see God in every being and thing. Literally. Make a conscious effort to do this in a very real way right now. Treat everybody and everything as you would treat God. After a couple of hours of this you might feel God intoxicated. Do this exercise often. Pretend that God's hiding in everyone and everything, playing hide-and-seek with you.

    How does this meditation practice change your perspective?
    How does this exercise make you feel?
    Could you live this way all the time? Why?

- Another quote for reflection comes from the *Quaker Book of Wisdom* by Robert Lawrence Smith:

"We need more silence in our lives, more stillness in our homes. We need, in our increasingly complex and frenetic world, to silence ourselves - and to listen."

How comfortable are you with silence?
What does being "still" mean to you?

COOPERATIVE DRAWING CARDS TEMPLATE

COOPERATIVE PUZZLES

This game is a spin off from a favorite game of our family named "PIT." However, this game requires cooperation instead of competition. If you have the time, try both a competitive round and a cooperative round. Be sure to process how the rounds felt differently and how the results were vastly different.

OBJECTIVES: Teamwork, cooperation/competition, sharing, planning, and decision making

   NEEDS:
- Identical, 4" x 6" blank puzzles for each participant (see template or purchase them at a craft store)
- A baggy for each player

 FACILITATOR NOTE: Number the backs of the pieces of each puzzle. For example, the first puzzle would have the number 1 on each of its ten pieces. The second puzzle would have the number 2 on each of its pieces, etc. When you have labeled all of the puzzles, mix up all of the pieces and place an equal number of pieces into a baggy for each player. The purpose is for each team member to put his/her puzzle together by sharing pieces openly rather than keeping them for themselves.

PROCEDURE: Invite the players to sit in a circle, and give each of them a baggy full of puzzle pieces. Explain that the purpose of the game is for each player to collect a matching puzzle. Invite the players to take out all of their pieces and lay them number side up, in front of them.

 Explain that when it is their turn, each player can look around the circle and choose to trade any matching set of puzzle pieces they have for the same number of matching pieces from another player. For example, if player **A** has a pair of threes and a pair of fives, he/she may decide to trade the threes with player **B** who has a pair of fives, so that **A** will now have four pieces of number five. Two important rules: the trade pieces must always have matching numbers and AT NO TIME CAN A PLAYER REFUSE A TRADE.

One trade occurs for each turn. Play continues until each player has a complete puzzle.

 FACILITATOR NOTE: It may be important to remind the team that the goal is for everyone to have a complete puzzle and that trades may seem difficult to the individual, but could help the team complete the goal.

 VARIATIONS:
- You can set up the challenge by stating that the idea is to see how quickly the team can accomplish the goal.
- Asking them to complete the goal in silence is also a great variation, then allowing them to talk in the second round and see how much faster they can go.
- You can also choose to do a competitive round where everyone trades at the same time, which becomes very chaotic, loud, and fun! In the competitive round, you call out the number of tiles you are wanting to trade and everyone does it at the same time. You can be selective and not trade with someone if you think it won't be in your best interest.

 SPIRITUAL INSIGHT: When did our world become so competitive? Some would say from the very beginning, and that it is in our nature to be self-centered. Perhaps it has become a conditioned response to a society that thrives on competition. However, within the human heart is the capacity to love unconditionally, to have compassion without limits, and to place the good of the world ahead of self-centered goals. The challenge is to live in a self-centered world with a community-minded heart and soul.

 GOING DEEPER: Within the Islamic faith is a basic decision making process - consultative decision making - called "shura." Shura is a process of discussion and exchange of thoughts by which two or more individuals come together to reach an agreement on an issue of mutual interest. Shura does not mean an absence of leadership. It means an absence of dictatorship.

> "Those who hearken to their Lord, and establish regular prayer; who (conduct) their affairs by mutual consultation; who spend out of what we bestow on them for sustenance." Al-Qur'an 42:38

Shura is practiced at every level of Islamic life, from a small family to the highest level of governance. Islam encourages the tremendous benefits of synergy and the spirit of consensus as one of the qualities of the righteous.

> Questions:
> How are decisions made in your family, school, classroom, group?
> What is meant by true consensus?
> Is it easier to abide by majority rules, compromise or true consensus?
> How does competition get in the way of building community?

Have you ever had to make an unpopular decision?

 GOING **W**IDER: In the Going Deeper section, we highlighted an Islamic tradition. We encourage you to examine other world religions for their views and practices on community and compassion.

Here are some ideas:

- In the Quaker tradition a decision-making meeting is known as a "clearness meeting." The guests ask open-ended questions rather than give advice. Their role is to keep you looking at all the possibilities until you begin to see your way clear to a decision. Such "meetings" may open up avenues that you had not considered possible or point out alternatives that you had not explored.
  (*Getting it Together*, by C. Wehrheim)

- The Mennonite Tradition uses the process of community-based consensus. The strong foundation of their decision-making principles has greatly impacted the way the world mediates.

- Buddhists see differences among groups, etc. as temporary and secondary to interdependency and common ground. Consider how this philosophy differs from the way others process their conflict.

COOPERATIVE PUZZLE TEMPLATE

DEPENDING ON YOU

This is the quintessential Raccoon Circle initiative. Tim first learned this initiative while spending a day at Jim Cain's home in New York for a workshop in 1999.

OBJECTIVES: Creating community, cooperation, team safety, and communication

NEEDS:
- One 12' - 15' webbing circle tied with a water knot (see Appendix B). It is VERY important to reference the proper procedure for tying a water knot.

PROCEDURE: Have 6 to 10 participants (for larger groups, use a water knot to add in more webbing) gather around the webbing circle and hold the circle with both hands about a shoulder's length apart, forming a circle.

SAFETY TIP: Tell the group that each person is responsible for the safety of the group. This is accomplished when participants use slow movements and work to follow each other.

Ask participants to begin placing some tension on the webbing circle. Slowly have participants increase the pressure on the circle by leaning back. Tell them the goal is to achieve balance while supporting each other.

Explain to the group that this balance is only accomplished when they can depend on each other. When everyone is working together, a high degree of support is possible. But when someone has a different agenda, is hurt, or chooses not to be cooperative or align themselves with the group's goals, each person is affected. At this point give a tug on the webbing circle from your position (try this gently at first so you know how the circle reacts). Everyone will feel your interruption of the balance. Explain that even those on the complete opposite side felt what happened. Sometimes we would like to think our actions only affect ourselves when in fact each person on the team or in the group is affected.

Depending on each other requires trust and communication. Turn to the participant on your right and left, tell them you need to step away for a moment and ask them to help compensate when you do. Slowly begin to release your tension, allowing it to be picked up by the participants on both sides. Usually this can happen with almost no discernible change for the rest of the participants. Explain that when we are open, honest and communicate with each other, things happen more smoothly.

Next, tell the group you are ready to step back in and resume your place.

If you feel your group is ready for it, invite them to move in unison to a half sitting position and then back to standing. Try that a couple of times and then move on to a sitting position (as if in a chair), then back up. This illustrates that you can depend on each other in times of need.

PROCESSING QUESTIONS:
1. Do you understand your team's interdependence?
2. Did the "ripple effect" surprise you when the leader pulled the webbing?
3. Did you trust the team enough to really risk leaning back?
4. How did this activity remind you of relationships in your everyday life?
5. What did this activity teach you about yourself? Others?

 SPIRITUAL INSIGHT: The use of the circle as a sacred symbol is universal. The circle symbolizes many different relationships. One of the most sacred is the relationship between the creator and creation. When we are at one with the creator, our life has harmony, balance, and wholeness. The circle also encompasses the important relationships we have with each other on our journey. When we speak of our close "circle" of friends, we refer to those with whom we share the most intimate moments of life. The challenge is to recognize the meaning and importance of our relationship with the creator and those who walk with us.

GOING DEEPER: Within the Native American tradition, the circle is a sacred symbol. The circle represents many truths, one of the most valuable is that each life is a beautiful part of the Universal Circle to which we are all connected. The following words are taken from the writings of Black Elk.

> "Then I was standing on the highest mountain of them all, and round about beneath me was the whole hoop of the world.

"And while I stood there I saw more than I can tell and I understood more than I saw; for I was seeing in a sacred manner the shapes of all things in the spirit, and the shape of all shapes as they must live together like one being. And I saw that the sacred hoop [circle of tipis in the village] of my people was one of many hoops that made one circle, wide as daylight and as starlight, and in the center grew one mighty flowering tree to shelter all the children of one mother and one father. And I saw that it was holy.

"You have noticed that everything an Indian does is in a circle, and that is because the Power of the World always works in circles, and everything tries to be round. In the old days when we were a strong and happy people, all our power came to us from the sacred hoop of the nation, and so long as the hoop was unbroken, the people flourished. The flowering tree was the living center of the hoop, and the circle of the four quarters nourished it. The east gave peace and light, the south gave warmth, the west gave rain, and the north with its cold and mighty wind gave strength and endurance. This knowledge came to us from the outer world with our religion.

"Everything the Power of the World does is done in a circle. The sky is round, and I have heard that the earth is round like a ball, as so are all the stars. The wind, in its greatest powers, whirls [tornadoes]. Birds make their nests in circles, for theirs is the same religion as ours. The sun comes forth and goes down again in a circle. The moon does the same, and both are round. Even the seasons form a great circle in their changing, and always come back to where they were. The life of man is a circle from childhood to childhood, and so it is in everything where power moves. Our tepees were round like the nests of birds, and these were always set in a circle, the nation's hoop, where the Great Spirit meant for us to hatch our children."

 FACILITATOR NOTE: We've included the entire quote. You may wish to paraphrase this for a younger audience.

Nicholas Black Elk (Hehaka Sapa) was a Lakota Sioux of the Oglala band, born in 1863. He was a revered elder, medicine man and shamanic healer who began to have visions at the age of nine. His father's name was Black Elk, as was his grandfather and great-grandfather. Black Elk was second cousin to the great Crazy Horse who visited him often and whose death he witnessed as a teenager in September, 1877.

John Neihardt, a poet from Nebraska, recorded Black Elk's story in *Black Elk Speaks* which was published in 1932. This book remains today as the best-known Native American biography. The legacy of Black Elk lives on in the traditional culture of his grandchildren.

Questions:
    In what way do circles have importance in your culture?
    How does nature help you to understand the Creator?
    What is the most powerful experience you have had in nature?

Do you feel connected to all living creatures? If so, how? If not, why not?
What impresses you most about what Black Elk had to say?

GOING WIDER: In the Going Deeper section we highlighted a Native American belief.
We encourage you to examine other world religions for their views on the circle as a
sacred symbol.

Here are some ideas:

- The Celtic people and the Druid priests created beautiful artwork in the form of
  never-ending knot designs that can be seen in their ancient texts. This art
  represents the unity of all things, the never-ending circle of life and nature, and
  the connection between every living and existing thing. They show the never-
  ending spirit in all things.

  How have you seen the never-ending circle illustrated in your life?
  What impact does this realization have on you?

- In Taoism the yin/yang symbol is illustrated by two equal sides that come together
  to form a complete circle. The dark yin side and the light yang side meet together
  and create a single force of energy, one unable to exist without the other. Tai Chi
  Ch'uan, a Taoist exercise sequence, focuses on bringing the energy (physical and
  spiritual) of the body into balance and a rhythmic flow. The yin/yang symbol
  represents the required balance of body and spirit, movement and stillness,
  masculine and feminine, inside and outside.

  If you are a practitioner of Tai Chi (if not, invite one to your group for a mini
  session), introduce your group to the Tai Chi walk and the possible feelings of
  energy and balance that can be attained using this discipline.

  How do you see the opposites of yin and yang coming together in your life?
  Share a time when you had to take the good with the bad.
  How does this recollection make you feel?

- Check out the Labyrinth Section in this book. It illustrates yet another way that
  the circle is a powerful symbol of faith.

FACE TO FACE/BACK TO BACK

This comes to us from our daughter, Bethany, who served as an intern at the Tucker Leadership Lab, High and Low Ropes Course in Liberty, Missouri. It is one of her favorite icebreakers. It is good for low risk sharing and enables the facilitator to begin seeing the trust level of a group.

 OBJECTIVES: Personal sharing, breaking down barriers, communication, creativity

PROCEDURE: Have the group stand in a circle with one member in the center. The members in the circle should number off one, two, one, two, etc., making pairs. The pairs should then face each other, turning their backs to the pairs on either side of them. The result is that the group members in the circle are face-to-face and back-to-back. Once everyone is standing facing their partner, the person in the middle gives the group a question to share with their partner. Encourage them to ask something creative, that they would feel comfortable answering about themselves. As the pairs finish sharing, they should turn back-to-back with their backs touching.

When everyone has turned, the person in the middle calls "FACE TO FACE AND BACK TO BACK." At this point, everyone must find a new partner, not the person they are facing and not the person they have already shared with. The person who has been "it" finds a new partner. The person who is left without a partner will now be "it." This continues until everyone has had a chance to share with all the other group members.

PROCESSING QUESTIONS:
1. How did you decide who to share with when it came time to switch?
2. What did you learn about someone in the group?
3. How do you feel differently about the group now?
4. What was the most challenging aspect of this initiative?
5. What does this activity remind you of?

 SPIRITUAL INSIGHT: Many times in life we make assumptions about others with very little information. We judge others by how they look, talk, dress and/or act. We sometimes allow these judgments to cause us to miss the opportunities to get to know many of God's children. The challenge is to stay open to those who are different from us. Only when we allow ourselves to change our opinions of what is acceptable, and accept what is given, can we understand that everything and everyone has value.

GOING DEEPER: Within the Native American culture there is a well-known and often-quoted proverb, "Never judge a man until you have walked a mile in his moccasins." This expression lifts up the concept of not judging someone until you understand their perspective. We cannot fully understand another person until we have lived through their experiences. This understanding stresses the need for empathy, rather than judgement or sympathy.

> Questions:
> What false assumptions have you made about others in the past? What influenced your decisions?
> What assumptions have others made about you? How did that make you feel?
> Why do we judge each other?
> What is the difference between sympathy and empathy?
> How do you give life to this proverb? At home? At school? In this group?
> How does this change the way you look at others?

 GOING WIDER: In the Going Deeper section, we highlighted a Native American proverb. We encourage you to examine other world religions for their views and practices on acceptance and empathy.

Here are some ideas:

• The Baha'I faith strives for peace through the unity of all mankind. They do not accept intolerance and do not judge other's spirituality. The Baha'I believe in uniting all humankind. They draw from many of the world's faith traditions, believing the history of humankind runs in circles beginning with the first prophet, Adam.

"You are the fruit of one tree and the leaves of one bunch." Baha'u'llah

> How does this philosophy of the Baha'I faith affect your beliefs?
> How could this belief affect your life?

• Here is a story of one of the "desert fathers" who were the Christian Monks of the fourth century. They secluded themselves from society to practice humble living and become closer to God in preparation for his coming.

> "A brother in Scetis committed a fault. A council was called to which Abba Moses was invited, but he refused to go. So the priest sent someone to say to him, 'Come, for everyone is waiting for you.' So Abba Moses got up and went. He took a leaking jug and filled it with water and carried it with him. The others came out to meet him and said, 'What is this, father?' Abba Moses said to them, 'My sins run out behind me, and I do not see them, and today I am coming to judge the errors of another.' When they heard these words, they said no more to the brother, but forgave him."

What does this story say to you?
How can you apply it to your life?

- Have the group reflect on this statement from the Hindu guru, Sai Baba:

"Do not judge others, for when another is judged, you yourself are condemned."

When have you felt unfairly judged?
Is it ever appropriate for you to pass judgement on someone else?
   Why? Why not?
How has passing judgment on another person affected your life?

HERDING KITTENS

A variation of "Balloon Crossing" from Karl Rohnke's *Funn Stuff, Volume III*, this is a blast to watch! It is fun to see the different personality types interact. You might want to give extra challenges to those in the group who like to "take charge," so others get the chance to step up to the plate. If you are outside and it is windy, this could take all day!

OBJECTIVES: Teamwork, problem solving, leadership/followership, and FUN!

  NEEDS:
- Hundreds of balloons in a variety of colors. Well, okay, at least three balloons per participant (one per person if you are in a very large group, or two to three if you are in a smaller group).
- Enough webbing circles for each color of balloon used

PROCEDURE: Distribute various colors of balloons throughout the group. Ask each person to blow up their balloon(s) and tie off the neck so that it is close to the size of the one you are holding. After the laughter, miscellaneous raucous balloon sounds, excited conversation, and inevitable breakage, announce the Herding Kittens Challenge!

At GO, the group should try to move and arrange the balloons into groups by color, with the webbing circles serving as corrals. The balloons cannot be held or thrown, only batted by hand (no foot work here). Karl tells of seeing this accomplished by over 600 people in an auditorium with bolted down chairs!

Do not tell the group beforehand where each color balloon must end up. That is up to them. This is a timed event and considering that you will probably not get a chance to try this a second time, whatever time they establish will be a new world's record!

PROCESSING QUESTIONS:
1. How did the group get organized?
2. Who stepped into a leadership role?
3. What were the challenges to this activity?
4. How many times did your strategy have to change?
5. Was it difficult or easy to change in "mid stream"?

 SPIRITUAL INSIGHT: Our lives are sometimes filled with chaos. How we bring order to the chaos is the challenge. One spiritual discipline is to become the "non-anxious presence" in the midst of anxiety. Being the calm, centered spirit in the midst of what seems to be a storm can be a blessing to all those you come in contact with. Being able to maintain a non-anxious presence will keep you connected with the person and not their emotions. Being that calming influence shows a depth of faith, trust, and confidence in knowing that in the end, all is well.

 GOING DEEPER: The practice of meditation in Zen Buddhism has been passed on from generation to generation for 2,500 years. At the very heart of Zen meditation is Zazen. Zazen is the study of the self and how to release one's worries. Zen meditation seeks to reduce a person's suffering by helping one to slowly and methodically gain more power of the mind and to set aside anxious thoughts. It is an effort to be calm and keep negative emotions from driving us into a panic. Zazen invites us to look carefully for the ways we are attached to concepts, self-images, people or things that bring on our suffering. It is an effort to learn to laugh at ourselves for the many things we worry about. The Zen meditator is attached to the idea that gaining control of the mind and releasing its worries and anxieties can reduce suffering. This concept is illustrated in the following Zen parable:

"A man traveling across a field encountered a tiger. He fled and the tiger chased after him. Coming to a precipice, he caught hold of the root of a wild vine and swung himself down over the edge. The tiger sniffed at him from above. Trembling, the man looked down to where, far below, another tiger waited, looking up. Only the vine sustained him. The storyteller continues: A mouse, little by little, began to gnaw at the vine. The man saw a luscious strawberry near him. Grasping the vine with one hand, he plucked the strawberry with the other. How sweet it tasted!"

The great Master Dogen said, "To study the Buddha Way is to study the self, to study the self is to forget the self, and to forget the self is to be enlightened by the ten thousand things." To be enlightened by the ten thousand things is to recognize the unity of the self and the ten thousand things.

Questions:
How can the study of oneself be enlightening?
How can meditation help you overcome the craziness (chaos) of the world?
What does it take to be grateful for the strawberry?
How do we find balance between worrying about the ten thousand things and understanding how we are united with the ten thousand things?
How do you cope with worry?

 GOING WIDER: In the Going Deeper section, we highlighted a Buddhist practice. We encourage you to examine other world religions for their views and practices on meditation and prayer.

Here are some ideas:

- In many religious traditions, mantras are used in meditation. A mantra is the repetition of a word or phrase to help you focus.

    Catholics use rosary beads and repeat the Hail Mary Prayer and the Lord's Prayer, among others.

    In the Hindu tradition, Mala beads are often used for prayer and meditation. Some examples of a traditional Hindu mantra are:

        Praise to God, Hail to God
        Hail, Hail to God.

        All evil vanishes from life for those
        Who keep the sun in their hearts.

    You can make up your own mantras to help you meditate and change them as often as you like. Something as simple as: God is love, or Love is the reason, can help you keep focused.

        What are some ideas you have found helpful for meditating?
        Share some ideas for mantras.

- A quote for the group to contemplate and discuss:

    "You do not have to leave your room. Remain sitting at your table and listen. Do not even listen: simply wait. Do not even wait. Be still and solitary. The world will freely offer itself to you unmasked. It has no choice. It will roll in ecstasy at your feet." Frank Kafka

        What does this quote say to you?
        How does it make you feel?
        What practices do you use to enhance your meditation (or quiet) time?

HOLY MACKEREL

This game is an adaptation of one that comes from Tucker Leadership Lab in Liberty, Missouri. It centers on group coordination and communication. It is a great game to introduce the importance of goal setting.

OBJECTIVES: Goal setting, communication, problem solving, and teamwork

NEEDS:
- A tarp (or a sheet or piece of plastic) with different size holes cut in it (the smallest should be just bigger than a tennis ball, the largest as big as a big pancake)
- You will also need a tennis ball

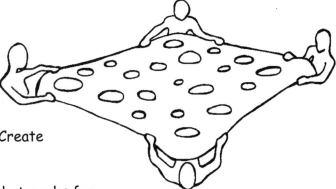

PROCEDURE: Each 8' x 12' tarp can accommodate about 15 people, so if your group is bigger than 15, use a bigger tarp. Have the team gather around the tarp. Tell them that they have to earn points to achieve a goal. Create a story/metaphor that fits your team.

FACILITATOR NOTE: Use a metaphor that works for your group. An example might be: You have been challenged as a group to raise money to "Save the mackerels." How can you be the top fund raisers?

The team must set a goal of how much money they want to raise and a strategy for raising that money using the tarp and tennis balls. Some of the things they must decide include:

- What the holes in the tarp are worth. (For example: the smallest hole is worth the most points; the largest hole the least points.)
- How many times they can toss the ball.
- The distance between the tosser and the tarp.

The challenge is to acquire the needed money by putting the tennis ball through the specific holes whose values will tally up to the total amount needed to "save the mackerels." When they have had a few tries and experienced some success, you might want to further challenge them by blindfolding a few members, or striking some of them mute.

PROCESSING QUESTIONS:
1. What strategies worked for your team?
2. What was difficult?
3. How did the team work together to achieve the goal?
4. Was there consensus, or did someone just decide?
5. How did this activity mirror how this team works in real life?
6. Did you come away feeling successful? How so?

SPIRITUAL INSIGHT:
Spiritual growth doesn't happen by chance. We grow spiritually when we are intentional. Sometimes we limit our growth by being closed-minded to new ideas or concepts. We grow most when we challenge ourselves to move out in faith. However, many times we do not understand or accept new ways of viewing God or our own spirituality. The challenge is to be a lifelong learner of how God is working in the world, and to not be limited by the viewpoint we begin with.

GOING DEEPER:
Thich Nhat Hanh [pronounced "teek naught hawn"] is a Vietnamese Buddhist monk. During the war in Vietnam, he worked tirelessly for reconciliation between North and South Vietnam. He lives in exile in a small community in France where he teaches, writes, gardens, and works to help refugees worldwide. Thich Nhat Hanh has been living in exile from his native Vietnam since the age of forty. He has championed a movement known as "engaged Buddhism," which intertwines traditional meditative practices with active nonviolent civil disobedience. Although his struggle for compromise meant he had to relinquish his homeland, it won him accolades around the world. One of his thirteen precepts states:

"Do not think that the knowledge you presently possess is changeless, absolute truth. Avoid being narrow-minded and bound to present views. Learn and practice non-attachment from views in order to be open to receive others' viewpoints. Truth is found in life and not merely in conceptual knowledge. Be ready to learn throughout our entire life and to observe reality in yourself and in the world at all times."

Questions:
   What is the hardest part of learning a new idea or concept about God or
      spirituality?
   In what ways are we raised to believe we possess the absolute truth?
   Does being open to new ideas mean we are weak in our faith?
   How do we limit our spiritual growth by not appreciating other's views?
   What is the difference between truth found in life and conceptual
      knowledge?

GOING WIDER: In the Going Deeper section, we highlighted a Buddhist concept. We encourage you to examine other world religions for their views and practices on seeking truth and spiritual growth.

Here are some ideas:

- It can be challenging to open your eyes and mind to new ideas, but that is the first step to deepening your spiritual life. Open your heart and mind and discover that knowledge never ends. In seeking spiritual growth you must admit that there is more to learn and therefore you must open your eyes to see, open your heart to experience, and open your mind to learn. You are always beginning again.

> "I'm a monk, and the strangest thing happened in my monastery. We had a visit from the Buddha. We prepared for it, and gave him a very warm welcome. He stayed overnight, but he slipped away early in the morning. When the monks woke up, they found graffiti all over the cloister walls. Imagine! And do you know what he wrote? One word-TRIVIA-TRIVIA-TRIVIA- all over the place.

> "Well, we were in a rage. But when I quieted down I looked about and realized, 'Yes, it is true.' So much of what I saw was trivia, and most of what I heard. But what is worse, when I closed my eyes, all inside was trivia. For several weeks this was my experience, and my efforts to rectify it just made it worse. I left my monastery and headed for the Magic Monastery.

> "The Brother showed me around. First, the Hall of Laughter. Everything fed the flame of laughter, big things and small, sacred, solemn, inconsequential. Only laughter there.

> "Next, the Room of Sorrow. The very essence of bitter tears - those of the bereaved mother, the lonely, depressed. Only sorrow here.

> "Now the Hall of Words. Words upon words, spoken and written. Alone they must have had some sense, but all together - total confusion. I cried out, 'Stop! Stop!' but I was only adding words to words.

> "Next, the great Hall of Silence. Here there is no time.

> "He finally took me to the Hall of Treasures. 'Take anything you want,' he whispered.

> "I chose the heart of Jesus, and with it I am heading back to my monastery."

> from *Tales of a Magic Monastery* by Theophane the Monk

What does this story say to you about spiritual growth?
How would you have felt finding that someone you trusted in your
house had put graffiti all over the walls and then left?
What would you have done?
What have you experienced as a result of opening your mind?
How do you feel when you learn something wonderful unexpectedly?

- While we readily accept truth in other areas - the law of gravity, the rules of
mathematics - we'd like to pick and choose when it comes to spiritual truth. The
Bible makes it very clear that we do not determine truth, but rather that we
discover truth.

"Then we will no longer be like children, forever changing our minds about
what we believe because someone has told us something different or
because someone has cleverly lied to us and made the lie sound like the
truth. Instead, we will hold to the truth in love, becoming more and more in
every way like Jesus..."   Ephesians 4:14-15

How do you recognize truth?
What are some truths you have discovered?
How has the truth impacted your life?

If Ever...

This can be a powerful activity for groups to examine hurtful behaviors or attitudes. Bullying begins at an early age and its scars can last a lifetime. This experiential piece can be a door to open dialogue about how it feels to be bullied or to have bullied someone. A great opportunity for forgiveness.

  OBJECTIVES: Connectedness, reconciliation, friendship, and acceptance

PROCEDURE: This activity is best done with the participants silent. Have the group stand in a circle and follow the directions:

If you have ever. . .	Then . . .
been laughed at. . .	take one step out.
been made fun of. . .	take one step out.
been called names. . .	take one step out.
had your feelings hurt. . .	close your eyes.
felt alone. . .	turn out.

Pause 10 seconds.

If you have ever. . .	Then . . .
stuck up for someone. . .	take one step back in.
smiled at a stranger. . .	take one step back in.
made a friend. . .	open your eyes.
hugged someone who needed it. . .	step in.
forgiven someone. . .	hold hands with person next to you.

We are all human, we have been hurt by others. We may have been hurtful to others, but each of us has the power to forgive, reach out and move on. Take a moment to share with the others in the circle how you feel about them.

PROCESSING QUESTIONS: First, ask the group to find another person to share with. Then bring everyone back to a large group for processing:

Small group:
1. Share times when you have reached out, smiled, forgiven.
2. Share a time when you were laughed at, picked on, hurt.

Be sure to take turns in the sharing process.

Large group:
1. Why do we hurt each other?
2. What is harder, to forgive or ask forgiveness?
3. What keeps us from reaching out?

 FACILITATOR NOTE: This activity has the potential for the disclosure of deep feelings. Be prepared to help participants express those feelings in an atmosphere of acceptance and safety. You may need to allow additional time for processing.

 SPIRITUAL INSIGHT: Connectedness is one of the deepest needs in our human existence. But because of the fragile nature of relationships, we often find ourselves disconnected and in need of reconciliation. Learning to truly reconcile our differences will enable us to experience connectedness and true community.

 GOING DEEPER: The sacred text of Islam, the Qur'an, uses the term "ummah" to refer to the community of believers. The term is used to describe individual communities, both great and small as well as the worldwide community of believers. In Islamic social theory, the ummah is formed from the threefold consensus of its members: consensus of mind, consensus of heart, and consensus of spirit. In the Qur'an (2:143) it is referred to as "Umma Wasat," the middle nation, a unique component of the Islamic community which has been asked to maintain equitable balance between extremes, pursue the path of moderation, and establish the middle way. Such a community of Muslims is intended to be a model for the whole world to emulate.

Questions:
How does the concept of ummah enhance what you have heard about the nation of Islam?
What does it require to have consensus in a community?
Have you ever been a part of a community you felt at one with in heart, mind and spirit?
What does it mean to maintain balance between extremes?
How does consensus encourage reconciliation?

 GOING WIDER: In the Going Deeper section, we highlighted the Islam faith. We encourage you to examine other world religions for their views and practices on reconciliation and forgiveness.

Here are some ideas:

- Have your group reflect on this Hindu scripture from the Ramayana:

  "A superior being does not render evil for evil. A noble soul will ever exercise compassion even toward those who enjoy injuring others."

  What does this scripture say to you about reconciliation?
  What does it take to keep this kind of attitude toward others?

- Jesus taught: "Love your enemies and pray for those who persecute you, so that you may be sons of your Heavenly Father. For he makes the sun rise on evil men as well as good men; and sends the rains to unjust men as well as just men."

  We are not being asked to approve of what our enemies do. If we return evil for evil, then things can only get worse; but if we meet evil with goodness, then the situation may miraculously be transformed for the better. God forgives all of us because God is unconditional love. To know this healing love, we too must forgive all those who we believe have wronged us.

  Who is your enemy?
  How do you feel about your enemies?
  What does unconditional love mean to you?

INNER COMPASS

Adapted from the activity, "Hansel and Gretel," in the book entitled *Quicksilver* by Karl Rohnke & Steve Butler, this initiative is useful to help groups understand the concept of perceptions. In this activity, the goal seems easily attainable but can be quite tricky. Often, the group not participating but watching is able to grasp the concept quickly.

OBJECTIVES: Directional challenge, team cohesion, peer pressure, and problem solving

NEEDS:
· Enough brightly colored balls (or markers) to mark the group path (one ball for approximately every five steps the group takes, often twenty to thirty balls)

PROCEDURE: This game requires a large area in which to move around. Begin by explaining the following rules to the group:

1. The team's objective is to move from point A to point B. Point B is a preselected destination around thirty yards from point A.
2. One team member is selected as the contact person – the one to make contact with point B.
3. The entire team must have and maintain physical contact with one another at all times.
4. The group must move from point A to point B with their eyes closed. The contact person should be aware of where point B is before closing his/her eyes. Make sure eyes remain closed even after stopping.
5. During the journey, the facilitator should see to group safety while a second person is assigned to follow the group and drop a ball every four or five steps, to mark the path the group takes.
6. When the team thinks they have arrived, or when they have meandered long enough that you choose to stop them, ask them to each point to where they believe point B is located, then have them open their eyes.

PROCESSING QUESTIONS:
1. Did you ever feel the need to move in a different direction from the group?
2. Did you feel right in the direction the group was heading?
3. How did the group decide which way to go?
4. Was your voice listened to?
5. How does this game mirror how this group functions in real life?
6. Discuss the phrase "Being popular isn't always right, being right isn't always popular."

SPIRITUAL INSIGHT: Throughout history, world leaders have made the choice to go against the popular "directions" of society. Martin Luther King Jr. responded to his inner compass when he made a nonviolent stand against racism. Mahatma Gandhi responded to his inner compass when he stood for the rights of his homeland against colonization. Mother Teresa followed her inner compass when she chose to live a life of poverty with the poor people of Calcutta. Each of us has the inherent ability to seek the divine in all things. The challenge is to develop our own inner compass which will enable us to determine our best course.

GOING DEEPER: Rabbi Yisrael Salanter, a great Torah leader in the 19th century, founded a school of thought called mussar, which emphasizes the psychology of spiritual practice. While reflecting on his life, he said:

"In adolescence I aimed to change the world — to right the wrongs of humanity on a global scale. I envisioned an end to war, oppression, injustice, and strife. Soon I realized that I would have to change my own community first. Only after succeeding here, could I hope to impact upon the world. So I set out to improve education, mediate quarrels, and introduce proper priorities into local politics. Finally, I saw that my real work was with my family. I must begin by changing and perfecting those closest to me — my wife and children. Only later did I see that my true focus of effort must be myself — that to become a kind and decent human being was a life's worth of work. And if, with the grace and assistance of G-d*, I could succeed in this most difficult of tasks, I would be making the greatest of all possible contributions to my family, community, and even to the world."

*This is not a misspelling. Within the Jewish community, out of respect, one never writes the name "God."

Rabbi Hillel said: "If not now, then when? If not here, then where?"

Questions:
What do you dream of doing in your life?
How do great people become great?
Where do we have the most influence in our lives?
What does the phrase "think globally, act locally" say to you?
If you could do anything without the fear of failing, what would you do?

GOING WIDER: In the Going Deeper section, we highlighted a Jewish philosophy. We encourage you to examine other world religions for their views and practices on the inner compass and being fully present in the moment.

Here are some ideas:

- Give your group a task to accomplish. At a random point during this task say aloud to the group, "Right now!" Have the group stop what they are doing and center themselves in the immediate moment and space they are in and respond to you with the same words: "Right now!" It can have the impact of a strong hit of caffeine to the spiritual system. Don't delay your life any longer. Right now is your time!

   What are you waiting for?
   What can you do to begin living in the moment?
   How could living in the moment impact your life?

- Ask the group, "Where am I?" (The answer you are looking for is "Here.")
   Ask the group, "What time is it?" (The answer you are looking for is "Now.")
   Wherever you go and whatever time it is by the clock...it is always here and now. In fact you will begin to see that you can't get away from the here and now.

   What does living in the here and now mean to you?
   How can living this way impact your life?
   How can you make this practice a part of your life?

- Have the group reflect on this quote by Thich Nhat Hanh:

   "So we must go back to ourselves, and when we have joy and peace in ourselves, our creations of art will be quite natural, and they will serve the world in a positive way."

Our appointment with life is in the present moment. If we do not have peace and joy right now, when will we have peace and joy?

NUMBERMANIA!

This game challenges the group to be critical thinkers. They need to work together and use problem-solving skills. As a facilitator, set reasonable goals and then give grace when needed. Tim used this as an experiential activity in one of his MBA classes and the instructor loved it!

OBJECTIVES: Teamwork, problem solving, communication, cooperation, critical thinking, logic and reasoning

NEEDS:
- A webbing circle or rope to lay out a 10' by 20' boundary
- Discs or markers that have the numbers 1 through 30 drawn on them. Gym spots work great. However, we've also used paper plates secured with florist pins
- A stopwatch is also helpful

PROCEDURE: Distribute the markers throughout the field of play with evens on the left side and odds on the right side. Do this randomly, so it is not obvious to the group as they approach the field. (See diagram.) Gather the group at a distance of approximately 20' from the field of play so they are not able to study the placement of the numbers. Explain that the object is for them, as a group, to gather around the field of play, but not to enter the field.

When you say go, one team member at a time may step inside the field on a number and then step out. Their goal is to sequentially step on all the numbers beginning with one and going to thirty. They have 10 minutes or three attempts to see how quickly they can complete the task. Between attempts, the group must move away from the field of play to strategize on how to improve their time.

PROCESSING QUESTIONS:
1. How well did your team strategize and use the ten minutes?
2. What helped your team improve its time?
3. What feelings did you experience in attempting this initiative?
4. Did your team listen to all suggestions?
5. How did your team come to agree on strategy?
6. How did your team utilize the available resources?

7. Was everybody involved in the strategizing?
8. What did this activity remind you of?

 VARIATION: Remove the #13 spot before the activity begins. Add the following processing questions:

How did you handle the challenge of the missing number?
What happens when things don't go as planned?

 SPIRITUAL INSIGHT: Sometimes life's challenges seem overwhelming at first glance. We look at obstacles in our life and ask, "How will I ever get through this?" We sometimes forget to take a step back and breathe. Allowing ourselves to gain perspective by stepping away also gives us a chance to see God in the challenge. God is in all things and can work through challenges to help us grow and develop.

 GOING DEEPER: In our increasingly hectic world we must make time to see God, experience God and seek him out. In Carol Werheim's book, *Getting It Together*, she tells about connecting with God anytime we want or need to with a "breath prayer." Breathing in and out, you repeat words that you have chosen as a small prayer. You can do this anytime, anywhere, without anyone even being aware of it. When you feel like you need to connect with God, whether out of frustration, fear, or pure joy, say a breath prayer and recognize that God is always available.

Have the group practice saying a breath prayer. (For example, "I thank You, God, for this most amazing day.") Have the group say or think the first part of the phrase (I thank You, God) as they breathe in. Then, as they slowly exhale, say or think the last part of the phrase (for this most amazing day). Remember that a breath prayer can change from moment to moment. It is as simple as sending your present thought to God.

Questions:
What are some times when you could use a breath prayer?
What are some breath prayers that come to mind?
How could saying breath prayers affect your life?

 GOING WIDER: In the Going Deeper section, we highlighted a Christian prayer practice. We encourage you to examine other world religions for their views and practices on seeing God in all things.

Here are some ideas:

· A wonderful poem by e.e. cummings can generate some great discussion:

"i thank You God for this most amazing day;
for the leaping greenly spirits of trees
and a blue true dream of sky;

for everything
which is natural which is infinite which is yes"

    What happens when you look for God in all things?
    Have your group make up a verse about seeing God in everything.

- Have the group reflect on this saying by an ancient Egyptian sage, Hermes Trismegistus:

    "He is hidden yet obvious everywhere.
    He is bodiless yet embodied in everything.
    There is nothing which he is not.
    He has no name because all names are his name.
    He is the unity in all things,
    so we must know him by all names and call everything God."

    What does this quote say to you?
    How does it make you feel?
    How does it motivate you?

NUMBERMANIA! DIAGRAM

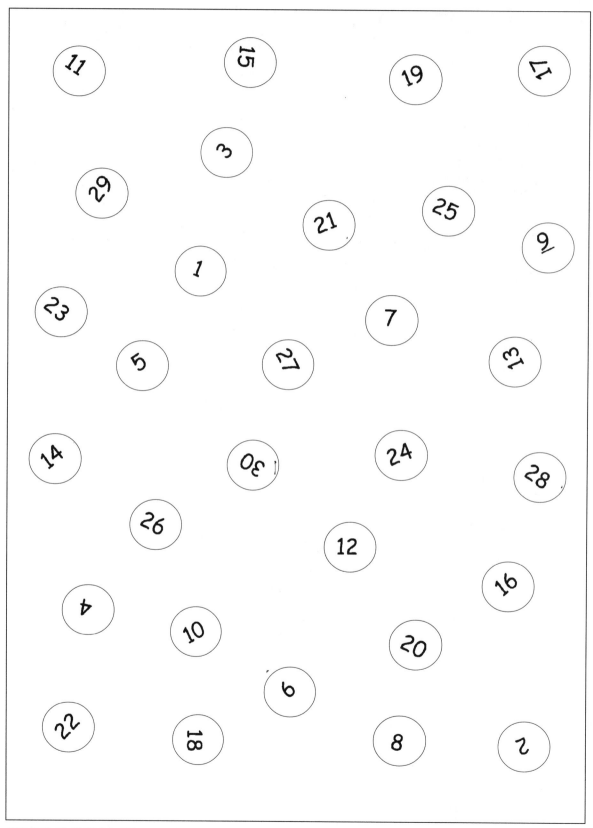

ORB-IT

This is yet another variation of the popular initiative commonly referred to as Raccoon Circles. This game emphasizes the need for everyone to be involved.

OBJECTIVES: Team unity, dealing with adversity, flexibility, the dangers of looking out for ourself in a cooperative environment, and trust

NEEDS:
- 12' to 15' of webbing tied with a water knot to make a circle. Be sure to reference the proper procedure for tying a water knot (see Appendix B). This is VERY important.

PROCEDURE: Gather your group and tell them the object of the game is for the group to create the shape of a circle with the webbing you are about to give them and for them to maintain it as a circle. Each member must maintain two-handed contact with the webbing at all times unless otherwise directed.

Give the group the webbing and have them begin. Once each member has joined in, and has placed their hands on the webbing, look to see if the group has formed a well- shaped circle. Encourage them to do their best job to create a well-formed circle. Once this is accomplished, encourage the group to begin creating some pressure on the circle to see how tightly they can pull on the webbing.

SAFETY TIP: (Safety is very important in this game. Encourage each participant not to do things that might endanger the whole group such as letting go with one hand, jerking the webbing, letting go quickly, etc.). Have the group safely experiment with how one movement affects the whole group. Discuss how they must depend on each other for safety. Also make the point that just one person can adversely affect the whole.

Now comes the tricky part. Begin to remove participants from the circle one or two at a time, and tell them to remain outside the circle. Each time you remove a participant, encourage the group to maintain the circle. Reinforce that the objective is to maintain a perfect circle. It will quickly become difficult to maintain a circle once you have fewer than five participants left. As you get down to three or fewer, it becomes impossible to maintain a circle.

PROCESSING QUESTIONS:
1. How did losing members of the team affect the circle?
2. What is the hardest part of depending on others?
3. When did the objective become impossible?
4. How did it feel to be outside of the circle and unable to help?
5. How did it feel to be holding the webbing and unable to maintain the circle?
6. What did this activity remind you of?

 SPIRITUAL INSIGHT: Sometimes circumstances change and we have difficulty accepting the new reality. When life changes unexpectedly, we can spend lots of energy fighting the circumstances or practice the art of spiritual surrender. Spiritual surrender is the art of letting go and accepting life for what it is, not what we hoped it would be.

 GOING DEEPER: "Letting go and letting God" is one way of saying it. "Not as I will it, but as You will it."

The Taoists call this "going with the Tao." This requires us to let go of how we think it should be and just let things be. It does not imply that we become apathetic or inactive in our lives, but that we simply recognize the need for surrender to a higher power and make that choice. This realization usually doesn't come until we are finally exhausted with trying to bend life to meet our own desires. It is easy to fall into the trap of thinking we know what is best for ourselves and everybody else - especially those we love and care about. By surrendering control of our lives and letting go of those around us, we allow God to work.

There is great spiritual freedom in surrender. Freedom from blaming others or feeling guilty. Freedom from anxiety, for we cannot change our fate. Freedom from ambition, for we achieve nothing on our own. Freedom from dissatisfaction, because everything is the will of the Higher Power.

"God demands nothing less than complete self-surrender as the price of the only real freedom worth having." Mahatma Gandhi, Hindu spiritual leader.

Questions:
Share a time when you let go and let God. How did it make you feel?

In what ways have you experienced spiritual freedom?
What does giving up control mean to you?
What keeps you from letting go and letting God?
Who's really in charge anyway?

 GOING WIDER: In the Going Deeper section, we highlighted an Eastern religion philosophy. We encourage you to examine other world religions for their views and practices on surrender and selflessness.

Here are some ideas:

- Have the group reflect on this Sufi teaching story:

    A man knocked on God's door. "Who's there?" asked God from within. "It's me," said the man. "Go away then. There is no room for two," said God. The man departed and wandered in the arid desert until he realized his error. Returning to the door, he knocked once again. "Who's there?" asked God as before. "You," answered the man. "Then come in," God replied.

- God's plans for us are always for good. Unknown plans can be frightening, but when the plans belong to God, we can rest assured that we can expect the best.

    "For I know the plans I have for you," says the Lord. "They are plans for good and not for disaster, to give you a future and a hope."
    Jeremiah 29:11 (The New Living Bible)

Even when bad things happen we can rest in the hope of God's love for us and that ultimately His plans do work for our good.

    What does this scripture mean to you?
    How could it impact/change your life?

 FACILITATOR'S NOTE: Be aware of group members who may be dealing with a traumatic issue and the anger with God that may be a result. God is big enough to handle our anger.

PASSAGES

This classic initiative has been enhanced by many practitioners; notable contributors include Karl Rohnke and Chris Cavert. In this adaptation, we have added safe zones and a message of encouragement to those who reach the goal. Once again, it takes some setup time and a few props, but the experience can be powerful and is worth all the effort.

OBJECTIVES: Communication, trust, listening, teamwork, cooperation and patience

NEEDS:
- Enough space to set up your field of play
- Masking tape or rope to establish boundaries
- Webbing circles or hula hoops to establish safe zones
- A variety of objects to be set up on the ground (hanging from the ceiling if you're inside) to serve as obstacles. We suggest two chairs with a string tied between them to increase the level of challenge. Sometimes we create a higher challenge that provides a shortcut to see how many will go for the tougher but shorter journey.
- A jar or container with a lid that closes, containing messages of success and encouragement. These can be personalized with names on each one if you so desire. Generic messages are fine, but be mindful of the age appropriateness, for your group. (See the template of sample messages for ideas.)
- Blindfolds for half of the group

PROCEDURE: Pair up students in any way you choose. Explain that the objective is to have the sighted partner guide the blindfolded partner through the field of play and to the container of messages without touching any of the objects. (If the blindfolded partner touches anything they must begin again.) The more obstacles the better. The sighted partner who is standing outside the field of play is not allowed to touch the partner or enter the field during the activity. They can only verbally guide their partners to the goal.

 SAFETY TIP: Explain that there are safe zones for the blindfolded partner to enter if they need to take a stimuli break. However, they must remain blindfolded until they reach the goal.

When the partner has successfully opened the container, drawn out a message and moved off the field of play, they become the guide to their partner. Encourage them

to take their partner on a different route than they traveled. Let them repeat the challenge if time allows and if they would like.

PROCESSING QUESTIONS:
1. What was difficult about the activity?
2. How did partners communicate? Did it work?
3. What did you learn about communication?
4. How did the guide feel when their blindfolded person touched an object?
5. Was the trust level affected after the blindfolded person touched an object?
6. How did guides respond when their partners touched an object?
7. What feelings came up during the activity?
8. Was there any goal setting done before the activity?
9. What was it like to achieve or not achieve your goal?
10. What did the message from the container mean to you?

 SPIRITUAL INSIGHT: The world can be a dangerous and scary place and at times we feel blinded by our lack of understanding. It is to our benefit to learn to accept the guidance of another as we make our journey. How does our walk with God compare to this activity? Do we sometimes long to hear God give us direction or advise us on which path to chose? How do we hear God's guidance in our lives?

 GOING DEEPER: From the Christian Old Testament comes the words of Solomon:

"Trust in the LORD with all your heart, and do not lean on your own understanding. In all your ways acknowledge Him, and He will make your paths straight."   Proverbs 3:5-6 (New International Version)

In order to understand the depth of this scripture, it is important to know that for the Hebrews the phrase "with all your heart" meant totally and completely. So to paraphrase this verse it would sound something like this: Rely on God completely and do not try to figure out everything on your own. Understand that in this world, things don't always turn out the way we'd like. Even if we don't understand, even when we can't see what God sees, we can depend on God. We can choose to trust God.

Questions:
What is the most difficult part of trusting God?
How can you believe in something you can't see?
What gets in the way of hearing God in your life?
What does the phrase "with all your heart" mean to you?
Have you ever felt abandoned by God?
Have you ever suddenly realized God's direction and support in your life?

GOING WIDER: In the Going Deeper section we highlighted a Christian scripture. We encourage you to examine other world religions for their views and practices on trusting and listening.

Here are some ideas:

- Have the group reflect on the words of the Hindu sage, Swami Chetananda:

    "When you are with someone you love very much, you can talk and it is pleasant, but the reality is not in the conversation. It is simply being together. With God you don't need to say a thing - it is just great to be together."

    How does your time alone with God make you feel?
    How does this help you see God as directing your life?

- Being quiet helps us to hear God's voice. God often expresses his powerful love in gentle whispers. Listen for God's whisper.

    "'Go out and stand before me on the mountain,' the Lord told him. And as Elijah stood there, the Lord passed by, and a mighty wind storm hit the mountain. It was such a terrible blast that the rocks were torn loose, but the Lord was not in the wind. After the wind there was an earthquake, but the Lord was not in the earthquake. And after the earthquake, there was a fire, but the Lord was not in the fire. And after the fire there was the sound of a gentle whisper. When Elijah heard it, he wrapped his face in his cloak and went out and stood at the entrance of the cave."

    I Kings 19:11-12

    What does God sound like when you listen?
    When and where do you listen for God?
    When and where do you hear God?
    How do you relate to this story?

MESSAGES OF ENCOURAGEMENT TEMPLATE
Adapt messages to fit the age of your group.

- -

To enjoy the flavor of life, take big bites. Moderation is for monks.
Robert Heinlein

- -

It is better to wear out than to rust out.
Anon.

- -

In humor there is truth. You need to take humor more seriously.
Ralph Nader

- -

Play isn't a reward for working. It's homework for living.
Mark Roth

- -

There is only one of you in the world, just one.
And if that is not fulfilled, then something has been lost.
Martha Graham

- -

Yesterday is history. Tomorrow is mystery. And today is a gift.
Loretta Laroche

- -

Adapt the pace of nature: its secret is patience.
Ralph Waldo Emerson

- -

In the middle of every difficulty lies opportunity.
Albert Einstein

- -

You can't steal home and keep your foot on third base.
Herbert V. Prochnow

- -

People's true wealth is the good they do in this world.
Mohammad

- -

To be conscious that you are ignorant is a great step
toward knowledge.

Benjamin Disraeli

- -

excerpts from *Experiential Quotes: Words of Wisdom to Live and Work By* compiled by Todd Miner & Simon Priest

A PEACEABLE WORLD

This art-based activity is wonderful on a sunny day when you can go outside and make a mess. It is great indoors on a rainy day with lots of paper towels, too! This is one of those activities where you don't need to give as much direction as you might want. Let the group and their creativity lead the way.

OBJECTIVES: Team work, creativity, envisioning and discussing

NEEDS:
- One flat twin sheet for every 5 to 6 participants
- Water-based paint (red, yellow, blue, black and white)
- Stakes to secure the sheet to the ground (this is best as an outside activity)
- Paper plates to use as paint "holders"
- Lots of water for clean up - wet wipes work well
- A suitcase

PROCEDURE: Have the group sit in a circle and place the suitcase in the middle. Explain that they are going on a journey. As a group they are traveling to a new planet.

This planet is called "The Totally Peaceful Planet" and each person can bring one item with them—but it isn't going to fit in a suitcase! They will need to choose a feeling, a concept, or an idea to bring along. (You may choose to offer suggestions like "love, harmony, tolerance, music, family...") What would the Totally Peaceful Planet need from our world? Solicit their responses as you move around the circle.

Once you have gone around the circle, ask the group to form teams of five or six. Explain that they have 30 minutes to create a mural which represents their image of a peace-filled world.

Now inform them that they have a "canvas" and paint but they may use only their hands and feet to apply the paint. At the end of the time allowed have everyone dispose of plates and empty paint bottles, and then get cleaned up while the art work dries.

Once everyone is cleaned up, give each team the opportunity to share their project with the community.

 VARIATION: You will need one T-shirt per participant (or have everyone bring a T-shirt) and T-shirt paint in several different colors. Have the T-shirts laid out in a line to create a long canvas. The goal is to create one big picture (a panorama) using all the T-shirts. Each participant gets one minute per shirt to add something to the picture. To do this, have the participants line up in front of the shirts, one person per shirt. After a minute passes, call time and have the line move one shirt to the right with the last person going to the front of the line. Remind the group often that the goal is to create one big picture out of all the T-shirts, when laid side by side.

(This idea comes from the activity, "T-shirt Panorama" from *Place of Connection* by Jackie Gerstein.)

PROCESSING **Q**UESTIONS:
Have the group discuss their ideas and the creative process as they share their project.
    1. How did it feel to "create" peace?
    2. Were you challenged to come up with only one item to take on your trip?
    3. What was it like to be limited to use only your feet and hands?

 SPIRITUAL **I**NSIGHT: Peace is a universal concept! Every language in the world has a word or phrase which represents the concept of peace. Peace is sometimes defined as the absence of war; however, the Hebrew word for peace, "Shalom," represents a broader definition, one that embraces peace as serenity, harmony, justice, and hope. Shalom is the act of making peace within our lives, with each other, and with God. How can we become the peacemakers in a world longing for true shalom?

 GOING **D**EEPER: To speak of Judaism without the word shalom is like trying to discuss American Democracy without using the Declaration of Independence. It's that central to the faith. Often the Hebrew word "shalom" is translated into the English word "peace." But it is more linguistically related to the root word meaning "wholeness," the opposite of fragmentation, shattered dreams, and broken hearts. Even when it means peace, shalom is far more than the absence of war. It is the presence of peace, wholeness and fulfillment.

    Questions:
        What does the concept of peace mean to you? Do you think of the absence
            of war or a more shalom definition of fulfillment and wholeness?
        What does justice mean and how is it related to peace?
        In the Old Testament of the Bible, peace is depicted with a lion and a lamb
            sitting down together. What does this say to you about peace?
        How would you define the role of peacemaker?
        What keeps the world from finding lasting peace?

GOING WIDER: In the Going Deeper section, we highlighted a Jewish concept. We encourage you to examine other world religions for their views and practices concerning peace.

Here are some ideas:

- People of all spiritual traditions seek peace, within themselves and for our world. Many dedicate their lives to promoting peace.

  What does the word "peace" mean to you?
  What is your definition of a peacemaker?
  Who comes to your mind as one of the greatest peacemakers of all time?
  Give an example of someone you know personally who is a peacemaker.
  How does s/he inspire you to become a more active peacemaker?
  How do you promote peace?

- Have the group reflect on the following "Prayer for Peace" by St. Francis of Assisi:

  Lord, make me an instrument of Your peace.
  Where there is hatred, let me sow love;
  Where there is injury, pardon;
  Where there is doubt, faith;
  Where there is despair, hope;
  Where there is darkness, light;
  Where there is sadness, joy.

  O, Divine Master,
  grant that I may not so much seek to be consoled as to console;
  to be understood as to understand;
  to be loved as to love;
  For it is in giving that we receive;
  it is in pardoning that we are pardoned;
  it is in dying that we are born again to eternal life.

  What have you done in your life to promote peace?
  What do you do on a daily basis to promote peace?
  How could you be a more active peacemaker?

SANTICKY, FANTICKY, LIM PO PO

This game was shared with us on our first trip to Russia. We were in a small camp setting about 500 miles south of Moscow in the Varonesh region. We gathered there with 35 Russian teenagers, all members of the Russian-American Friendship Club. They really enjoyed the new games and initiatives we introduced and wanted to teach us one of their favorite games.

OBJECTIVES: Community building, communication, and attention to detail

PROCEDURE: This game has three categories of participants:
1. The leader
2. The followers
3. The guesser

The leader's role is to not be discovered by the guesser as they lead the group in a series of body actions. The guesser's role is to determine who the leader is. The role of the followers is to help hide the leader. This is a "follow the leader" type of game, with a twist.

Form a large circle; ask for a volunteer to be the guesser. Have the guesser stand in the center of the circle with eyes closed. The facilitator then points to the person who will start out as the leader.

The leader repeats a simple body movement in time with the chant "Santicky, Fanticky, Lim Po Po." An example might be a jumping jack. The followers should imitate this movement. The guesser can open his/her eyes when the chanting starts. Next, the leader subtly changes the body movement and the followers immediately initiate the change. The trick is to do this as quickly as possible while the guesser attempts to figure out who the leader is.

It may take several attempts for the guesser to identify the leader. Once the leader has been identified, the leader becomes the guesser and the followers choose a new leader and the game begins again.

PROCESSING QUESTIONS:
1. What was it like to be the guesser?
2. What was it like to be the leader?
3. How do the followers impact the leader or the guesser?
4. If you could choose a role, which one would you want to be and why?
5. Which role has the most control?

 SPIRITUAL INSIGHT: Everyone is following after someone or something. Who or what are you following? Would the people around you be able to guess who you are following by your actions? Many people in the world profess to be a follower of some spiritual leader. However, their actions do not match the behaviors of that leader. A follower is one who works to be like the leader, to do as the leader instructs and to be a role model for others seeking to follow. Who are you following?

 GOING DEEPER: Matthew, a disciple of Jesus tells the following story:

"One day as Jesus was walking along the shore beside the Sea of Gallilee, he saw two brothers, Simon, also called Peter and Andrew, fishing with the rest, for they were commercial fishermen. Jesus called out to them, 'Come, be my disciples, and I will show you how to fish for people.' And they left their nets at once and went with him.

"A little further up the shore he saw two brothers, James and John, sitting in a boat with their father, Zebedee, mending their nets. And he called them to come, too. They immediately followed him, leaving the boat and their father behind."

> Questions:
> Have you ever made a decision to follow a spiritual leader? If so, how did you decide?
> Does your spiritual path lead you to behave in a certain way? If so, how?
> What price do you pay for following your spiritual leader?
> How would people know who you are following?
> Do actions really speak louder than words? If so, how?

 GOING WIDER: In the Going Deeper section, we highlighted a story from the Christian faith. We encourage you to examine other world religions for their views and practices concerning following.

Here are some ideas:

• You can follow after certain lifestyle principles - to be rich, to be famous, to be wise, to be committed. You can also follow a person; you can use him/her as an example and desire to be like him/her. Whatever or whoever you choose to follow will determine the quality of your life.

Where is the person you are following going, where are they headed?
How do you know you are following the right person/thing?
What sacrifices have you made to follow your heart?

- The Confucian idea of "superior person" is a concept of teaching by modeling and learning by imitation. By modeling virtuous behavior, we have an enormous impact upon others. For example: "Follow the way of bamboo, which models growth through resilience and the upward action of its shoots."

What are some other "nature" examples to follow?
What are you modeling?

SHOE HOLLER!

A fun and loud game to get everybody energized! It is more competitive than most, but that's okay! Be sure to take care in keeping everyone safe. This is a good icebreaker activity with low risk of personal disclosure.

OBJECTIVES: Communication, concentration, listening, problem solving, and following directions

 **NEEDS:**
- A webbing circle to accommodate a pile of shoes
- Blindfolds for half of the group

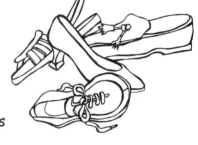

PROCEDURE: Place the webbing circle in an area where the group can create a large circle ten to twelve feet out from the web. Have the group divide into pairs, either by your choice or by letting them choose. Have everyone gently toss one shoe into the webbing circle.

 FACILITATOR NOTE: If you have those in the group who are extremely uncomfortable about removing their shoes, offer to have them use one of yours or a spare shoe you have brought with you.

Have one person in each group put on a blindfold. Then tell them they are to go into the middle and try to retrieve their partner's shoe. The sighted partner should be trying to assist by yelling directions. If they return with the wrong shoe, their partner must be blindfolded, take the wrong shoe back, and try to retrieve the other partner's shoe. The team with both correct shoes back on their feet wins.

 SAFETY TIP: Watch for bonking heads in the center. Have at least one spotter on both sides of the outside circle. Say a few words before starting about walking slowly and having bumpers up (keeping your hands up in front of you) while blindfolded.

PROCESSING QUESTIONS:
1. Was this task easier or harder than you expected it to be?
2. What made it difficult for you?
3. Could you distinguish your partner's voice above the rest?
4. How could you have improved on your time?
6. Was this activity frustrating for you?
7. Did your partner give you clear directions? How could it have been clearer?
8. What did you learn from your partner to improve your performance?

VARIATION: Have someone play the part of a distractor. This person should call false information to the blindfolded members, and try to keep them from accomplishing their goal. The distractor may use charm or humor, but is limited to words only. Some additional processing questions might be:

What was it like to be given the wrong information?
How difficult was it to block out the distractor and listen to your partner?

 SPIRITUAL INSIGHT: In life there are many voices competing to give us direction. How do we distinguish those who are speaking the truth from those who intend to deceive us? One way to know God's voice is to pray and meditate in silence. It is through frequent communion with God that we learn to recognize God's way of speaking to us. Taking time to remove ourselves from the hectic, chaotic world gives us the serenity of soul which enables us to hear God most clearly.

 GOING DEEPER: Within the Judeo-Christian scriptures we find the book of Proverbs, written by King Solomon. Proverbs 17:1 reads:

"Better a morsel of dry bread and tranquility with it, than a house full of feasting with strife."

In this proverb we are encouraged to seek tranquility and peace as our lasting wealth. The riches of the world can fade or be taken from us. But if we live with peace and tranquility, we have wealth that stands the test of time.

Proverbs 3:5-6 reads:

"Trust in the Lord with all your heart and lean not on your own understanding; in all your ways acknowledge him, and he will make your paths straight."

This proverb encourages us to seek God's guidance in all things and trust God will show us the path that leads to our happiness and a life of meaning.

Questions:
How do we learn to hear God's voice in our life?
What gets in the way of hearing God's voice?
How hard is it to trust in God, rather than our own understanding?
Do you seek peace or wealth? Can you have both at the same time?
What steps have you taken to find serenity?
How has God spoken to you in the past?

 GOING WIDER: In the Going Deeper section, we highlighted some proverbs from the Jewish/Christian faith. We encourage you to examine other world religions for their views and practices concerning discernment and focus.

Here are some ideas:

- Mahatma Gandhi turned everything he did into a spiritual practice. He adopted a life of voluntary austerity, even spinning his own basic clothing. Whether engaged in international politics or mundane chores, he exemplified what he taught: "Live simply so that others may simply live."

    What changes would you have to make in your life to "live simply"?
    How would your decision to live simply affect those around you?

- Once a religious leader asked Jesus this question: "Good teacher, what should I do to get eternal life?"

    "Why do you call me good?" Jesus asked him. "Only God is truly good. But as for your question, you know the commandments: Do not commit adultery. Do not murder. Do not steal. Do not testify falsely. Honor your father and mother."

    The man replied, "I've obeyed all these commandments since I was a child."

    "There is still one thing you lack," Jesus said. "Sell all you have and give the money to the poor, and you will have treasure in heaven. Then come, follow me." But when the man heard this, he became sad because he was very rich.

    Mark 18:18-23

    What does this story say to you?
    What are the things that are robbing you of life?
    How would it impact your life to give those things away?

STEPPING STONES

This is a variation of the popular gridlock initiative. In this version, we like the element of using stepping stones and the metaphor of the journey. This is also an adaptable game with a personalized message for the group.

OBJECTIVES: Teamwork, communication, applying group memory, and problem solving

  NEEDS:
• 30 to 40 stones (gym spots, rocks, paper, carpet squares, anything that will stay in place and can be stepped on safely will do)
• Index cards to spell out the word you choose to have as the journey's message
• Tape
• A marker
• A space large enough to create a 15' x 20' stone field (see diagram)

FACILITATOR NOTE: Determine the message you believe will speak to your group's current stage of development. Some examples might be PATIENCE, SHARING, COOPERATION, TEAMWORK, COMMUNICATION, TRUST, MOVING ON, LETTING GO. This message will be placed letter by letter under the markers in the pattern you choose to have the team traverse.

PROCEDURE: Set out the entire field of markers, and then lay out the message, charting the course, stone by stone. Generally, the movement should be forward, but it can go laterally, horizontally or diagonally, never backwards. Be sure to have a diagram on paper to give to the spotter with the correct course pattern laid out. Once the pattern is established and the field is ready for play, gather your group around the field.

THE SET UP: Explain to the group that they are on a journey to discover the message of the wise sage. On their journey, they have come upon a field of stepping stones. They see a sign above the field that says there is only one correct path through the field and that successfully finding the path will lead them to the message of the wise sage.

The first task is to select a group guide. This guide will be given the key to the path and must have integrity to hold the truth, but not give it away. It is the guide's responsibility to communicate if the choices are "correct" or "incorrect." Those are the only words the guide is allowed to say.

Once the guide is selected, inform the group that one by one they will be asked to help the group move forward on the journey. A volunteer is selected to choose the first stone. If the "correct" stone is chosen, then another step may be attempted. If an "incorrect" stone is chosen, that team member must leave the field and the next team member begins again at the beginning. This process is repeated until the field is crossed.

At the end of the journey, have the correct stones gathered by the last person coming through. Then have the team place the stones in order with the letters showing. These stones will spell out the message of the wise sage.

VARIATION:
If you have the extra time, mix the letters up and have the group unscramble them when the journey is complete.

PROCESSING QUESTIONS:
1. Did your group strategize before starting?
2. Did you ever make a wrong step on the journey?
3. What were the consequences for making a wrong step? How is this like real life?
4. If we learn from failure, why are we so afraid to fail?
5. Did you feel pressure when it was your turn to choose?
6. What did you discover at the end of the journey?
7. How does this message speak to the group? To you?

SPIRITUAL INSIGHT: The journey of life is full of twists and turns; it comes with surprises and disappointments. The challenge is to find within your soul the capacity to be at peace with whatever the road brings. While we cannot control many of life's situations, we can step out in faith. Faith means believing that God will be there in our time of need. How does life's uncertainty test our faith?

 GOING DEEPER: Matthew, a disciple of Jesus, tells us this story:

> Jesus insisted that the disciples get in the boat and go on ahead to the other side while he dispersed the crowds. He climbed the mountain so he could be by himself and pray. He stayed there alone, late into the night.
>
> Meanwhile, the boat was far out to sea when the wind came up against them, and they were battered by the waves. At about four o'clock in the morning, Jesus came toward them walking on the water. There were scared out of their wits. "A ghost!" they said, crying out in terror.
>
> But Jesus was quick to comfort them. "Courage, it's me. Don't be afraid."
>
> Peter, suddenly bold, said, "Master if it is really you, call me to come to you on the water."
>
> He said, "Come ahead."
>
> Jumping out of the boat, Peter walked on the water to Jesus. But when he looked down at the waves churning beneath his feet, he lost his nerve and started to sink. He cried, "Master, save me!"
>
> Jesus didn't hesitate. He reached down and grabbed his hand. Then he said, "Faint-heart, what got into you?'
>
> The two of them climbed into the boat, and the wind died down.
>
> Matthew 14:22-32, (The Message)

Questions:
When have you stepped out in faith?
What keeps you from stepping out in faith?
How do we develop faith?
When you have felt like you were sinking in life, who was there to reach
out and keep you afloat?
Would you have gotten out of the boat?

 GOING WIDER: In the Going Deeper section, we highlighted a story from the Christian Bible. We encourage you to examine other world religions for their views and practices concerning stepping out in faith.

Here are some ideas:

- Reflect on this quote by Rainer Maria Rilke from *Letters to a Young Poet*:

  "Have patience with everything that remains unsolved in your heart. Try to love the questions themselves, like locked rooms and like books written in a foreign language. Do not now look for the answers. They cannot now be given to you because you could not live them. It is a question of experiencing everything. At present you need to live the question. Perhaps you will gradually, without even noticing it, find yourself experiencing the answer, some distant day."

- Faith is more than just believing; it is being willing to stake your very life on what you believe. Faith in God says that we are willing to trust God with our very lives. In faith, we have the courage to face any fear, to risk rejection, ridicule, even persecution in order to travel the path that our heart is being called to follow. When we step out in faith, we experience God's power at work within us.

  How does my faith in God affect my relationship with him?
  How does faith change the way I live?

- Here is another thought-provoking quote for reflection, which comes from Soren Kierkegaard:

  "Where am I? Who am I
  How did I come to be here?
  What is this thing called the world?
  How did I come into the world?
  Why was I not consulted?
  And if I am compelled to take part in it,
  Where is the director?
  I want to see him."

- Here is one more quote that we couldn't resist adding:

  "When you come to the edge of all the light you know, and are about to step out into the darkness of the unknown, faith is knowing one of two things will happen: there will be something solid to stand on, or you will be taught how to fly."

                                                        Barbara J. Winter

  How important is faith to living?

TIN PAN, BANG, BANG!

This is Lisa's all-time favorite initiative. It is fun, somewhat competitive and serves as a great metaphor for how we live in community or cliques. The challenge is in keeping up the pace and not letting the game drag on and on.

OBJECTIVES: Community building, communication, and cliques

ANY SIZE | GSD

NEEDS:
- A metal sauce pan
- A large wooden spoon

PROCEDURE: Gather the group into a circle. Explain that the object of the game is to always be in a group. If you are left "out" of a group, you have to leave the game. The group size will be determined by the number of times the leader bangs on the pot, i.e. three bangs = groups of three.

SAFETY TIP: Keep the group from getting too competitive - no pushing or shoving. You may want to make this a "no touching" activity.

When you are ready to begin, select a number to bang (start with a number less than six). The large group should break up into smaller groups. Help stragglers find groups, check numbers and send stragglers to the "out" space.

To get the group ready for the next round, yell "Popcorn!" This means everyone jumps away from the group they are in and no one is touching. Start banging again! When you are down to two players, the game is over.

PROCESSING **Q**UESTIONS:
1. What was it like to be "out" of a group?
2. What was it like to be "in" a group?
3. Did anyone get shoved out of a group?
4. Did anyone get pulled into a group?
5. How is life like this game?
6. Where do we form groups in life?
7. How hard do we work to fit in?
8. How do you decide who will be part of your group?
9. How do you decide what group to be a part of?

SPIRITUAL INSIGHT: In our world today, we are faced with many cultures, religions, sects, creeds, and political parties who work to exclude those who are not "like" them. Although many spiritual communities embrace the idea of inclusion, the day to day practice of acceptance is much more difficult. Inclusion, kindness, and compassion go hand-in-hand and must be practiced personally. What we do to others, we do to God. Mother Teresa of Calcutta said that when caring for the dying and destitute, she just saw "Christ in all of his distressing disguises."

 GOING DEEPER: On one occasion, an expert in law stood up to test Jesus.

"Teacher," he asked, "what must I do to inherit eternal life?"

"What is written in the Law?" he replied. "How do you read it?"

He answered, "'Love the Lord your God with all your heart and with all your soul and with all your strength and with all your mind' and 'Love your neighbor as yourself.'"

"You have answered correctly," Jesus replied. "Do this and you will live."

But he wanted to justify himself, so he asked Jesus, "And who is my neighbor?"

In reply, Jesus said: "A man was going down from Jerusalem to Jericho, when he fell into the hands of robbers. They stripped him of his clothes, beat him and went away, leaving him half dead. A priest happened to be going down the same road, and when he saw the man, he passed by on the other side. So too, a Levite, when he came to the place and saw him, passed by on the other side. But a Samaritan, as he traveled, came where the man was; and when he saw him, he had compassion for him. He went to him and bandaged his wounds, pouring on oil and wine. Then he put the man on his own donkey, took him to an inn and took care of him. The next day he took out two silver coins and gave them to the innkeeper. 'Look after him,' he said, 'and when I return, I will reimburse you for any extra expense you may have.'

"Which of these three do you think was a neighbor to the man who fell into the hands of robbers?"

The expert in the law replied, "The one who showed compassion."

Jesus told him, "Go and do likewise."

Luke 10:25-37

Questions:
What do you think is the moral of this story?
Which character best represents you at this point in life?
Share a time when you have reached out to a stranger/neighbor in need. How did it make you feel?

GOING **W**IDER: In the Going Deeper section, we highlighted a Christian parable. We encourage you to examine other world religions for their views and practices on compassion and inclusion.

Here are some ideas:

- Ask your group to quote the "Golden Rule." Most of us have been taught the "Golden Rule" since we were children. Most of us have also figured out that it is a lot easier to say than to live. Imagine if everyone chose to live by this timeless proverb that is found in almost every faith tradition.

    How would it change our lives?
    How would it change our world?
    What keeps us from practicing this "rule"?

- His Holiness, the Dalai Lama, is the spiritual leader of Tibetan Buddhism. Until the Chinese occupation in 1959, he was also the ruler of Tibet. The Dalai Lama teaches compassion for all beings. He even preaches compassion toward the Chinese who are destroying his country and oppressing his people. Only love can transform horror and hate into harmony and reconciliation. The Dalai Lama teaches, "My religion is kindness." To be kind is to acknowledge that we are all one family, that we are "kindred," that we are all animated by the one Life Force.

    What is your definition of "kindness"?
    How would you fill in the blank: My religion is _____"?

- Have the group consider the following from *Whispers of Love* by Mitch Finely:

    Reflections

    The Christian doctrine
    Of the communion of saints
    Is simple, really.
    All it says is
    That once you buy the farm
    You still live on the farm.
    All it says is
    That those who have gone before us
    Are still with us.
    All it says is
    That past generations
    Still count
    And must be taken into account.
    In other words,
    We're all in this together.
    All of us.

TURNING OVER A NEW LEAF

This initiative is known by many names and has several applications. The title we have chosen works best when a group is ready to move into the goal setting stage. This can also work with individual goals. As with all initiatives, feel free to adapt and make it fit your group and your group's needs.

OBJECTIVES: Goal setting, problem solving, communication, and teamwork

NEEDS:
- A 4' x 5' piece of tarp for every 10 to 12 people
- A black permanent marker for each group

FACILITATOR NOTE: Set up this activity by introducing the phrase "Turning over a new leaf." Discuss how making changes in our lives requires dedication and hard work.

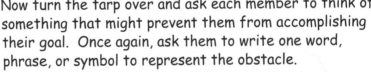

PROCEDURE: Ask each group to sit around their tarp. Have each member silently identify a change they would like to make in their lives. Give adequate time for everyone to identify their goal (change). On the tarp, have each member write one word, phrase or symbol that represents their goal.

Now turn the tarp over and ask each member to think of something that might prevent them from accomplishing their goal. Once again, ask them to write one word, phrase, or symbol to represent the obstacle.

At this point, ask the team to step on the tarp obstacle side up. Now challenge the team to turn over their "leaf." Everyone must maintain contact with the tarp at all times; no part of their body can be touching the ground around the tarp.

Added challenges might include no talking, half the group blindfolded, using only feet, etc.

PROCESSING QUESTIONS:
1. What was the most difficult aspect of this challenge?
2. Did you try something that didn't work? How did this make you feel?
3. How does this activity compare to making real changes in our lives?
4. What is the hardest part of sustaining change in our lives?

 SPIRITUAL INSIGHT: In each of our lives we are faced with endings and beginnings. Growth is only possible when we are willing to risk change. One of the most dramatic examples of transformation in nature would be the caterpillar who becomes a butterfly. In order to begin life as a butterfly, life as a caterpillar must end. In much the same way for us to become new, more vibrant people, we must allow change and transformation to begin.

 GOING DEEPER: In the Buddhist tradition, morning and evening services of chanting or worship take place in every monastery, temple, and home. With the placing of flowers and the lighting of candles and incense before a Buddha-image or some other symbol of the presence of the Buddha, monks chant together and the lay families offer a prayer. The flowers, beautiful one moment and wilted the next, remind the offerers of the impermanence of life; the odor of the incense calls to their mind the sweet scent of moral virtue that emanates from those who are devout; the candle-flame symbolized enlightenment.

There are special rituals to mark, protect, and bless the occasions of major life transitions. They publicly mark and protect times of passage from one status to another - times of unusual vulnerability such as birth, birthdays, coming of age, etc.

Questions:
What similar traditions/rituals do you practice?
How could traditions/rituals like this affect you?
What rituals help you through the transitions of your daily, spiritual life?

 GOING WIDER: In the Going Deeper section, we highlighted a Buddhist tradition. We encourage you to examine other world religions for their views and practices on change, endings and beginnings.

Here are some ideas:

• Nature is one of the greatest spiritual teachers of all time. We are a part of nature and by communing with the natural world, we can experience many awakenings. Trina Paulus' book, *Hope for the Flowers*, is a metaphor from nature that tells how Stripe and Yellow, two caterpillars, turn into butterflies.

Yellow had seen another caterpillar spinning a cocoon and asked, "If I decide to become a butterfly...what do I do?"

"Watch me," came the reply. "I'm making a cocoon. It looks like I'm hiding, I know, but a cocoon is not escape. It's an in-between house where the change takes place...During the change, it will seem...that nothing is happening, but the butterfly is already becoming. It just takes time."

Yellow had been afraid, but she took the risk and spun her own cocoon, later to emerge and unfold her wings.

> What does this story say to you?
> Share a time when you were in the cocoon stage of life. How did it feel?
> How did it affect your spiritual life?

- God and nature are full of symbols that mediate grace and move us toward change. The caterpillar, chrysalis and butterfly are a powerful metaphor.

Supply the group with a large white posterboard or piece of paper per individual and color markers. Have them draw a butterfly that represents their spiritual life. Have them use colors or draw patterns/symbols that represent how different aspects of their spiritual lives have grown. "Your soul is your greatest work of art."

> What does the metaphor of the butterfly say to you?
> How does your butterfly represent the beginnings and ending that have been
>   part of your spiritual life?
> What other aspects of nature have impacted your spiritual life?

- Have the group reflect on the following quote from T.S. Elliot:

> "We shall not cease from exploration
> And the end of all our exploring
> Will be to arrive where we started
> And know the place for the first time."

>> Reword this quote in your own words.
>> What is Elliot saying to us?

You Are on the Other Side!

Adapted from *The Book on Raccoon Circles* by Jim Cain & Tom Smith, this initiative requires team coordination and patience. It can also be FUN!

Objectives: Teamwork and problem solving

 Needs:
- Ten or more soft, throwable objects
- One webbing circle about 5' in diameter
- One webbing circle about 3' in diameter
- Enough untied webbing to form a boundary line 20' to 30' in length

Procedure: Create a boundary that resembles a meandering stream and place the smaller webbing circle about 20' from the nearest edge "inside" the stream. The larger webbing circle should be on the opposite side of the stream from the smaller one.

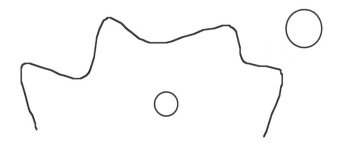

Select one member to be inside the smaller stationary circle; this person becomes the "tosser" and will be blindfolded. The tosser will need easy access to the throwable objects. The rest of the group will surround and hold onto the larger webbing circle. They are allowed to move around as a group, but they must stay on their side of the stream.

The setup that follows is only a suggestion; feel free to personalize it to make it fun for your group.

> "An ancient legend tells of a river filled with golden salmon with special healing powers. However, the water contains a dangerous and deadly virus that no human can survive. Inside this special river lives the blind Shaman. Legend tells us that when the Shaman hears the call: "Shaman, Shaman, hear our wish, send us out a golden fish!" the Shaman will toss a golden fish out of the river. However, the fish cannot be touched by human hands until it passes through the ring of friendship held by the group."

The object is for the group to call out to the blindfolded thrower on the other side helping to identify where they are so the thrower can try to toss one of the objects into their webbing circle. The receiving group can move (as a group) to try to catch the thrown object. The object cannot touch any of the members. If it does, it is considered an unusable resource. After each throw, the group must change positions along the shore line and call out again to help the thrower identify their location. This continues until all objects are thrown.

VARIATIONS: You can vary the game by tossing a certain number of objects from each selected location, changing the tosser and/or moving the shore line.

A more difficult variation requires the receiving group not to move their feet once the object has left the hands of the tosser.

Another favorite variation is to use only stuffed animals for the objects and require the receiving group to vocally emulate the animal sounds of the stuffed animal to be thrown. Have fun thinking of variations.

PROCESSING QUESTIONS:
1. How did it feel to be the tosser and be responsible for tossing the items?
2. How difficult was it to direct the tosser with only your voices?
3. How did the receiving team perform?
4. Were there strategies you tried that failed?
5. Did you experience any successes?
6. What would you do differently, now?

SPIRITUAL INSIGHT: Sometimes we think of prayer as a way of directing God in our lives, by asking God for what we think we need or bargaining with God or second guessing God. Prayer is much more than asking God for something. It is communion with God, conversation with God, getting to know God and opening yourself to Him. Praying does include sharing our deepest desires with God, but other key ingredients include thankfulness, confession, commitment, seeking direction, and just getting to know the heart of God. In a nutshell, prayer is communicating with God.

GOING DEEPER: Jesus taught us through his example that prayer makes it possible for us to have an intimate relationship with God who hears, cares, and is able to act. Jesus taught his disciples to pray what we refer to as "The Lord's Prayer." This has become one of the most common prayers in the Christian tradition:

Our Father, who art in Heaven, Hallowed be thy Name.
Thy kingdom come.
Thy will be done, On Earth as it is in Heaven.
Give us this day our daily bread.
And forgive us our trespasses,
As we forgive those who trespass against us.
And lead us not into temptation,
But deliver us from evil.
For thine is the kingdom, and the power, and the glory,
forever and ever. Amen

Questions:
What is prayer?
When/How did you learn to pray?
How is prayer a part of your spiritual life? Why?
What are some of the different ways of praying you have practiced?
Does God speak to you when you pray? How?
How has God answered your prayers?
When and where do you pray?

 GOING WIDER: In the Going Deeper section, we highlighted a traditional Christian prayer. We encourage you to examine other world religions for their views and practices on prayer.

Here are some ideas:

• The flame is a primary Jewish metaphor for the soul. Candle flames are the Jewish ritual representation of the nature of the soul. For example, it is customary to include prayer and a candle lighting ceremony on the Jewish Shabbat or holy days to symbolize how souls come closer together while enjoying sacred time and community.

Invite your group to have a candle lighting ceremony of their own. Light one or more candles that have been placed in a shoe box filled with sand for safety.

Have the group focus on the flames and repeat the sacred Jewish psalm: "In Your Light, We see Light, In Your Light." Reflect on your higher power and recite this psalm together slowly and thoughtfully. Have them sit for a while in silence before having them refocus on the group. As they begin to refocus on the group have them share the phrase with the others in the group: "In your light I see light."

How did this candle lighting ceremony make you feel?
How did it feel when sharing the phrase with others in the group?
What was new, or difficult, or awkward, or hopeful in the connection that
    happened through the verse?
What images, symbols or rituals do you connect with prayer?

· Introduce the group to the "Prayer of Just Being," also called contemplation. It requires you to simply do nothing and think nothing. It is especially helpful when you find that you simply cannot think anymore. This is the perfect prayer for those times when you have absolutely no creativity left, when you are stressed to the max.

Have the group sit in relaxed positions and focus their minds on nothing in particular. Encourage them to just relax into the deep peace and sense of well-being that only comes when connecting with their Higher Power.

What did you experience while contemplating?
How did it make you feel?
Have you used contemplation before?
What are the benefits of contemplation?

LABYRINTH

SECTION

TWO

THE LABYRINTH IS LIKE AN INVISIBLE THREAD
THAT CONNECTS US TO THE SACRED.

 # THE LABYRINTH

Tim and Lisa incorporate some exciting initiatives into their work with groups involving the labyrinth. It provides a variety of fun and exciting possibilities for groups of all ages and is a powerful tool used to bring about a deeply spiritual experience.

AN INTRODUCTION TO THE LABYRINTH

For the past ten years, the use of a labyrinth for meditation and as a symbol of the spiritual journey has gained popularity in North America. The power of the labyrinth to take the participant away from the noise and chaos of everyday life and into a quiet and reflective state draws thousands of eager "walkers" and involves a multitude of spiritual and secular settings. Labyrinths have been in existence on every continent of the world for over 3,500 years. They can be triangular or square, but most often they are round, starting from the outside and winding toward the center. The symbolic shape of the labyrinth has been found in places as diverse as England, Iceland, Peru, Egypt and India.

Many different metaphors are associated with the labyrinth, from the common Christian metaphor of the pilgrimage to the Holy Land to the journey of the unborn child in the womb. A labyrinth found in Crete contains 272 stones, matching exactly the number of days in the human gestation period.

The labyrinth is utilized by many different religions. One yearly celebration takes place on April 8th to commemorate the birth of Buddha. The labyrinth is walked with an offering of flowers placed in the center where sweet tea is poured over a statue of Buddha.

In Judaism, a labyrinth is sometimes walked during the celebration of Shavuot. This celebration marks the wheat harvest and the festival of first fruits. It is also the anniversary of the Torah being given at Mount Sinai. The labyrinth is walked while holding a representation of the Torah, symbolizing that the Torah belongs to every Jew, and all Jews must endure the journey.

Those unfamiliar with the labyrinth may in fact confuse it with the maze. The two are very different. The labyrinth has a unicursal path, meaning there is only one path in and that same path must be followed out to the original entry, thus making the entrance and exit one. The maze is full of twists and turns and many false paths that are meant to confuse the participant. In contrast, the labyrinth's path is unchangeable and predictable, meant to bring assurance to the participant that they need not worry about becoming lost.

Each time the labyrinth is walked, the experience is different. This variation reflects the truth of our spiritual development and journey. It allows us to fully enter into the process of reaching our spiritual center.

In group settings, the labyrinth can have a powerful effect on community, connectedness and a sense of companionship on the journey of life. We have used the labyrinth in camp, retreat and training settings with participants as young as six to those far older than 60! With some basic instructions, the labyrinth can be a very reflective, personal experience or one that has the entire group embracing and affirming each other along the way. We have included several suggestions for ways to utilize the labyrinth for your group's specific needs.

HOW TO BEGIN

To begin labyrinth activities with your group, determine what kind of labyrinth you want to build and how big you want to make it. We believe it can be exciting for the group to participate in the creation of the labyrinth and can enrich the whole experience. To start, you will want to familiarize yourself and the group with the shape of the labyrinth and how it is created. We recommend starting with a simple, basic style. For the purposes here, we suggest the classic seven-circuit labyrinth. Below is a diagram of how to draw the seven-circuit labyrinth, beginning with two lines intersecting in the middle. The seven circuits are then created by connecting the lines one circuit at a time. This tool can help your participants understand the shape of the labyrinth and the concept of "unicursal." Go through the drawing of the labyrinth with your group prior to creating an actual labyrinth, so they will have the big picture.

In addition to "life-sized" labyrinths, there are many hand-held versions. You may want to have participants create their own labyrinth out of paper, dough, wood, tile or other materials. This becomes a take-away keepsake of their time with the labyrinth. Once they have created a labyrinth of their own, it will be much easier for them to help build a big one and to understand the path they will be walking.

BUILDING THE LABYRINTH

Once you have a good idea of the basic shape of the labyrinth, it is time to consider dimensions. We have found that the path is best traveled when at least two feet are provided between circuits. This means a classic seven-circuit labyrinth will require a space at least 40 feet wide by 40 feet deep. If you are creating the labyrinth outside, you will want a flat area, so that participants do not need to worry about terrain. Inside, remember to allow enough room around the outside for participants to stand outside the labyrinth while waiting to enter.

Labyrinths can be made with different materials. We created a permanent labyrinth on a large canvas with paint. (This kind of labyrinth is available for rental through Forefront Ministries in Independence, Missouri.) However, to create a temporary labyrinth is easy and not too expensive. The cheapest way is to use masking tape on the floor of a multipurpose room! This can be a fine way to introduce the labyrinth, the materials are not as important as the activities. Outside, use florist's ribbon, without wire, like the kind you use to make those big yellow ribbons found on trees, and florist's pins. These can both be found in bulk at hobby or decorator stores. The florist pins are metal and in the shape of a "U" with two pointy ends. These work great to pin down the ribbon on grass, or soft earth.

To begin laying out the labyrinth, start with the middle and work through the diagram. This has proven to be the best procedure and helps the labyrinth stay in scale. You may need to adjust the circuits as you go, using a yardstick to maintain the width of the path throughout the process. We allow at least one hour to create the labyrinth. It can go faster, but surprises always occur!

WALKING THE LABYRINTH

Once the labyrinth has been constructed, it is time to prepare your participants for the journey. One school of thought suggests that you do very little to set up the experience. What we mean by this is simply let the labyrinth speak for itself. Give your participants just a few simple guidelines and then let them walk the labyrinth.

The first guidelines might include:

- Shoes are optional
- Walk in silence
- Do not touch others on the journey
- Spend as much time in the center as you like
- Don't rush the experience

After you have given the participants time to think about the experience, you might choose to have them work in pairs or threes to process the following questions together. Remember to allow the experience to be as public or private as each participant chooses, no mandatory sharing!

PROCESSING QUESTIONS:

- What did you expect going into the labyrinth?
- What stands out for you in your first walk?
- What do you want to remember about this experience?
- How did it feel to be silent for so long?
- Did you find the experience enjoyable, frustrating...?

AFTER THE FIRST WALK...

Once you have experienced the first walk, there are a number of focused walks you might want to consider. There are many ways to approach the labyrinth, from structured to what our daughter, Bethany, calls "Just shut up and listen!"

PROBLEM SOLVING WALK

The labyrinth can be used as a meditation tool for problem solving. In this activity you set up the walk by having each circuit represent a stage of problem solving. As they approach the labyrinth they should identify a situation in life that is causing them stress. This could be a decision they are facing, a difficult relationship or a situation they are unsure how to deal with. As they enter the labyrinth, have them follow the progression of steps outlined below:

About this concern...

Circuit	one	I think...
	two	I feel...
	three	The physical realities are...
	four	The spiritual aspects are...
	five	My relationships...
	six	My choices are...
	seven	Just listen.

On the way out...

Circuit	six	Envision the first step...
	five	See the vision...
	four	Be thankful for the answer...
	three	How does this impact my spirit...
	two	I feel...
	one	I think...

Once again, allow time for each participant to process individually and then with others in a structured way or informally. This can be a powerful tool for people, and having a chance to share the experience will be important for many.

AFFIRMATION WALK

One nice way to have the group walk the labyrinth together is to set up a walk of affirmation. Begin by having the group form a circle around the labyrinth and hold hands. Have the group look around them and begin to think about the positive attributes of the other participants. Explain that this time when they walk the labyrinth they are to be aware of the others on the journey. When they meet someone on the path, they are to greet each other and say something to affirm the other person.

They may choose to shake hands, hug or simply look into the eyes of the companion on the journey. Remind them that this journey will be longer than other times they have walked the labyrinth and that is okay. Do not rush the experience.

 # CELEBRATION DANCE!

This allows up to five persons to walk the labyrinth holding hands, negotiating the twists and turns together. We recommend music that is light and without words. Encourage an atmosphere of unity and celebration. Do not place structured expectations on this one; allow the groups to create their own experience.

LETTING GO WALK

For many of us there are relationships, issues, or past problems that we have trouble letting go of. This can cause us undue pain, guilt, or a myriad of other emotions. Sometimes this "baggage" weighs us down and keeps us from experiencing the joy of life. Set up this walk by passing around a bag or basket of small stones. Give each participant time to think about what they need to let go of in life. Encourage them to think of one word to symbolize this aspect of life they want to let go of. Give them time to "name" the rock. As they enter the labyrinth, give them the following structure to contemplate letting go.

Circuit		
	one	What do I think about letting go of this?
	two	What do I feel about letting go?
	three	How will this impact me physically?
	four	How will this impact me spiritually?
	five	What will letting go of this do to my relationships?
	six	What are my choices in letting go?

When they arrive in the center, provide a basket for them to drop the stone into, allowing them to physically let go. On the way out, the following is a suggestion for contemplating how letting go will impact them.

Circuit		
	six	How is my life different?
	five	What does this change look like?
	four	Express gratitude for being free!
	three	Spiritually this feels...
	two	Emotionally this means...
	one	Now I am ready to...

A possible **VARIATION** for this walk is to place a second basket in the center of the labyrinth. In this basket place cards with words printed on them that might include: Peace, Grace, Calm, Patience, Strength, Endurance, Assurance, Joy, Hope, Love, Faith, Integrity, Vision, Focus, Healing, etc. Be creative and open to the spirit as you write on the cards, or you might want to use the template provided on the following two pages. Make sure the participants know they are to let go of their stone and pick up a card. It is amazing how the universe provides a new gift to replace what we let go of willingly.

Provide time for the group to share what they let go of and what they received.

Letting Go Walk Template for Variation

grace	peace
calm	patience
strength	endurance
assurance	joy

hope

love

faith

listen

vision

integrity

healing

focus

FALLING APART: A WALK FOR DIFFICULT TIMES

This is a variation of a labyrinth walk from Donna Schaper's book *Labyrinths from the Outside In*, Skylight Paths Publishing, Woodstock, Vermont.

There are times in life when it seems that everything is falling apart. Nothing is going as expected. This time as the group members travel the labyrinth, have them imagine their journey inward and visualize the parts of their lives that are falling apart. Encourage them to allow them to fall. Have the group members metaphorically catch the pieces and gently lay them on the path of the labyrinth. Instead of trying to keep it all together, just let the parts fall where they will.

As the group walks the labyrinth, have them imagine that they are gently catching their falling parts and lowering them to the path. Encourage them to be thankful for the falling away. Be thankful for the chance to begin again, to choose what to pick back up and what to let lay.

During the time of meditation in the center of the labyrinth, have the participants consider rebuilding. They might ask for fresh insight and perspective - for renewed strength.

As group members begin their outward journey, have them gently pick up those parts that they have decided to take with them and tuck them neatly into their imaginary backpack. Tell them not to worry about the parts that they choose to leave behind. The metaphor of the labyrinth is always available for them to experience another day.

CONCLUSION

This section is meant to give you a taste of how exciting and meaningful the labyrinth can be to your group experience. There are limitless possibilities available within the labyrinth. One lesson we have learned is that no matter what we expect the labyrinth to bring to a group setting, it always exceeds our expectations.

CONTACT

SECTION

THREE

PLAY IS OUR BRAIN'S FAVORITE WAY OF LEARNING.

Diane Ackerman

 # CONTACT

This initiative, contributed by Kelly Ellison and Harlan Brownlee, is a powerful tool to increase trust and team unity. We have been in workshops where they have led CONTACT with youth, adults and intergenera-tional groups. The entire initiative takes at least two hours, and it is important to familiarize yourself with each of the six sections ahead of time. This initiative takes some up front work, but believe us, it is worth it! We want to thank Kelly and Harlan for sharing it with us.

CONTACT INTRODUCTION

Over the years, we have had the opportunity to develop a team-building process that is experiental by nature and allows new and existing teams the opportunity to establish or reestablish trust through cooperative movement. The movement exercises presented help break down barriers and open lines of communication. These six sequential movement activities are conducted in a supportive and encouraging environment where the participants develop new skills using movement as a means of communication and understanding.

Together the participants discover, explore, and develop a deeper trust and confidence in themselves and the other members of the team. Much of the material outlined here has been adapted from a form of dance entitled "Contact Improvisation." Contact improvisation or "Contact" is a duet form based on physical contact. Following the laws of physical motion the form includes a fluent range of weight giving and receiving, spirals and falls, touch qualities, and flow patterns. A contact improvisation dancer must be aware of the possibilities of the moment in order to create authentic movement and communication.

The role the facilitator takes in this type of training is essential and so we begin first by identifying the role of the facilitator. In this case, the facilitator must allow the process to unfold and permit the group dynamic to emerge. Facilitation is a way of providing leadership without taking the reins. A facilitator's job is to get others to assume responsibility and to take the lead. Your job is to demonstrate, observe, and empower your participants to discover a unique way to build trust and partnership skills. In this initiative, because we will be using structured improvisation, at times, it may seem like chaos, but that isn't the case. Trust us.

NEEDS:
• Music on either a tape or CD
• A tape or CD player
• A large room with no furniture or obstructions, suitable for moving in

FACILITATOR NOTE: We don't recommend this activity for over 50 people, unless you have additional facilitators to help you. IF possible, have the participants wear comfortable clothing, and we recommend that they do not wear shoes.

Select music that is sustained, smooth, and flowing. The upcoming movement excercises are best supported by simple graceful music. Be sure to review the music first. For the music, any of Enya's CD's work well, although, we have found "Watermark" to be the best. A more classical suggestion would be Pachabel's Cannon in D.

Memorize or make notes of the specific songs and their locations on the recordings that you will use during the workshop. Test the equipment before the workshop. You want to avoid standing in front of a room full of people while dealing with a technical glitch. Specifically, find the pause and start button. You'll use these many times.

PROCEDURE:

Begin by having everyone stand in a circle. Pose the following questions. Keep the answers short and to the point.

1. What does it feel like to be a member of an unsuccessful or dysfunctional team?
2. What does it feel like to be a member of a successful and functional team?

FACILITATOR DIALOGUE:

"Today we are going to give you an experience that will help you to better understand your role as a member of a team. We will accomplish this through a series of movement experiences (don't say the "D" word (dance); many people have preconceived ideas about dance and are afraid or will be too intimidated to participate) with partners and groups to help you better understand yourself and the members of your team. Are you ready?"

(If the group or organization has established a specified problem, i.e., trust among the team, this is a good time to generally mention the issue.)

SAFETY TIP: Inform the group that you will be watching out for their safety. Make it clear to the group that if you say the word "FREEZE," they must stop whatever they are doing until it has been established that everyone is safe.

"There are a couple of ground roles to follow: First of all, there is a possibility that you might be uncomfortable for a moment or two. Don't worry about what others are thinking. Everyone else will be too busy thinking about how they look and feel to worry about anyone else. Simply pay attention to how you feel in certain settings and just be aware of it – uncomfortable, embarrassed maybe, silly, like you're a kid again, but don't act on it. No judgements on yourself or others. In fact, just suspend any judgements for the next two hours. This exercise is nonverbal. Certainly, laughing and having fun is completely allowed, but no talking is to occur during the exercises. Are there any questions? Let's begin."

FACILITATOR NOTE: Remind the group that if their "uncomfortable" feeling goes beyond embarrassment (due to trauma or physical limitations, etc.) that it's okay to ask to be excused from the activity.

EXERCISE ONE: MIRRORING

FACILITATOR DIALOGUE:
"Everyone get a partner and spread out. Stand face to face with your partner. We will begin with a simple mirroring exercise. (Facilitator can get a volunteer and demonstrate mirroring.) It's called mirroring because your actions with your partner will mimic you as the mirror does. Like standing in front of the mirror with your reflection doing what you do, one person leads and the other follows. Between you and your partner, take a moment to establish who will lead and who will follow. Movements should be slow and intentional so that your partner can follow. Do your best to use slow gradual movements. Don't turn your back on your partner. Remember, your partner can't follow you if they can't see you. I am going to play some music, and I want you to listen to it and begin to move. Let the flow of the music guide your movement."

FACILITATOR NOTE: Give them a chance to establish the leader and follower, and begin the music. As the music plays, remind everyone to just move. No movement is wrong. Move around the room and help participants get started moving their arms, bending their knees, leaning forward and backward, etc. Encourage them to look around the room and see what others are doing; it's okay to copy.

FACILITATOR DIALOGUE: (After the first song)
"Change partners. Remember that you agreed to suspend judgment. If you are worried about how you look, just think about how weird everyone else feels about him/herself."

PROCESSING QUESTIONS:
1. How would you describe this experience in one word?
2. What did changing partners do to your initial comfort level?
3. How do men move differently from women?
4. Did you surprise yourself? How?
5. Did you know you could move that way?
6. Share some times when you've had to express yourself with motion.
7. Leaders, how was this experience for you?
8. Followers, how about for you?
9. How did you establish the leader and follower?

EXERCISE TWO: CHANGE IS GOOD

FACILITATOR DIALOGUE:

"Find a new partner. This next session of mirroring will be slightly different. Decide who will be the leader and who will be the follower. This time the facilitator will call out the word "change" throughout the music and when you hear this, you and your partner should change roles. Switch leads without any interruption to the flow of the movement. Let me demonstrate for you."

FACILITATOR NOTE: Begin slowly by saying "change" every 30 seconds or so, then gradually speed up. Eventually say "change" so frequently that the teams don't know who is leading and who is following. Explain to the participants that at this point, the goal is not to keep track of who is leading, but to let the flow of the movement guide your decisions. Working non-verbally, the partners must watch each other closely and stay together. The lead may change a number of times, but the changes should be so subtle that the participants may not always be certain who is leading or following. Let the third song finish playing before ending the exercise.

PROCESSING QUESTIONS:
1. How was that?
2. Anyone want to share what happened?
3. Did anyone get into a complete flow?
4. Did you lose track of who was leading and who was following?
5. Why do you think this movement exercise is important?
6. What did you learn about yourself?
7. What did you learn about your partner?

EXERCISE THREE: DIAMONDS ARE BEAUTIFUL

This exercise includes two sections of direct imitation. You will need to demonstrate with several volunteers.

SECTION ONE DEMONSTRATION:

Find a volunteer and ask him/her to stand directly behind you with about five feet between the two of you. See Diagram One below:

Wall or Boundary

Facing this direction **A** leads.

Diagram One

- Start the music.
- Partners face the same direction (see diagram).
- **A** begins by leading **B** in movement.
- **A** can move from side to side, forward or backward, etc., as long as **B** remains behind them.
- **A** passes the lead by turning either right or left 180 degrees, and facing **B**.
- **B** then takes the lead by turning either right or left 180 degrees ending up with **A** directly behind **B**, both facing the same direction.
- The partners can change leads as many times as the music permits.

SECTION TWO DEMONSTRATION:

Find three other volunteers and ask them to stand with you in a diamond shape. See Diagram Two below.

Wall or Boundary

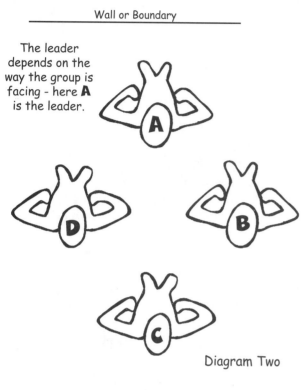

The leader depends on the way the group is facing - here **A** is the leader.

Diagram Two

- Start the music.
- Participants stand in a diamond shape facing the same direction. The direction the diamond is facing will determine the leader.
- **A** begins by leading the group in movement.
- **A** can move the group from side to side, forward or backward, etc. as long as they keep the spatial integrity of the diamond.
- **A** gives up the lead by turning either right or left 90 degrees and passing the lead to **B** or **D**.
- The lead continues to be passed by the leader turning 90 degrees.
- The group/diamond can change leads as many times as the music permits and reverse its order of rotation by changing leaders.

FACILITATOR DIALOGUE:

"Choose a new partner and decide who will lead. I will start the music. The lead partner should use smooth, flowing movements that the following partner can easily imitate. Remember you can pass the lead back and forth as often as you like. Be sure to keep the same distance between yourselves as you move to the music."

FACILITATOR NOTE: Have the participants move through section one of the exercise for about five minutes. Help the participants to make clear transitions when they change the lead. Encourage them to use smooth flowing movement that can be imitated easily. If there are any problems, demonstrate with a partner or group to clarify your point. As the partners or groups move, they will need to keep the same distance between themselves and their partners to maintain their spatial relationship to each other. The participants should realize that when they turn their bodies or faces, they are changing the lead.

PROCESSING QUESTIONS:
1. How was that increase in complexity?
2. This was much more complex than the first exercise. How did you feel following the leader in this exercise?
3. How was following different when the leader had his/her back to you?
4. How was it to be in the lead and not see the follower watching you?
5. What new perspectives does this give you about teamwork?
6. How does this influence your role as a team member?
7. How does it affect your role as a follower?

FACILITATOR DIALOGUE:

"Find a new group of four to work with in the diamond shape. Choose a leader to start. Be clear in passing the lead and remember to keep the same spatial distance as you move."

FACILITATOR NOTE: As the music plays, watch the change of lead between the partners in their diamonds. Keep an eye on the spatial integrity of the diamonds. Spend about five to ten minutes on this part of the exercise.

PROCESSING QUESTIONS:
1. Are you having fun yet?
2. How is your comfort level now vs. the first mirroring exercise?
3. How do you feel about the people around you?
4. Can you believe that you've given yourself permission to have this much silly, non-judgmental fun?
5. While leading, did you stop looking over your shoulder and do your own thing?
6. Is it easier to lead when you can't see the people following you?
7. How did you feel when it was time to pass the lead to someone else? Generous or reluctant?

Exercise Four: Trust Walk

Facilitator Dialogue:

"Are you ready to go to another level? During this next session we will go back to working with one partner; however, you will add a different type of communication, 'touch.' Partners will once again establish a leader and a follower. The key in this session is to never lose touch with your partner."

Demonstration:
Ask for a volunteer. Gently take the hand or touch the arm of your partner, and lead them around the room. Explain to the group that as the leader, you can touch your partner on the shoulder, arm, waist, or back, in a safe place. You can face them, be behind them, or walk with them, but you must always maintain contact with them. Be sure to show participants how they can change the part of the body they are leading to another part without losing contact. For example, many participants will lead with their hands. If they want to change from one hand to the other hand, they must first touch their partner with their second hand before releasing the first. You can also demonstrate how you can lead a partner with other parts of the body besides the hands. You can show them how to lead with your head, or arm, and even your leg.

Facilitator Dialogue:

"Choose a partner and decide who will lead and who will follow. As the music plays, the leader will gently guide the follower around the room. Remember to maintain touch at all times as this will be your only source of communication with your partner. Leaders, you are communicating by touch where you want to go and while you want to be firm, you also want them to be willing to follow you. Express yourself to your partner by moving up on your toes, bending your knees - be creative. When the music stops, you will stop."

Processing Questions:
1. As the leader, how did you communicate through your touch?
2. Were you being too rough or too gentle?
3. If you wanted them to stop, how did you do that?
4. As the follower, your job was to listen through touch. Was the person leading you gentle or abrupt?
5. Was the leader communicating clearly or did you feel confused about the directions?
6. How did you communicate to them that you were confused?

FACILITATOR NOTE: Begin the music again and have the participants work a few more minutes on the exercise.

PROCESSING QUESTIONS:
1. How was that? Leaders? Followers?
2. How are you feeling now? Guarded? Scared?
3. How did you feel at the beginning vs. the end of the sessions?
4. Is touching okay?
5. How did you improve communicating through your touch?

FACILITATOR NOTE: Have the participants switch leading and following roles. Start the music and have them continue to work on the exercise.

PROCESSING QUESTIONS:
1. How did it feel to reverse roles?
2. Did the followers do a better job of leading having had the experience?
3. Did the leaders do a better job of following having had the experience?
4. What did you do differently from the first time?

EXERCISE FIVE: TRUST WALK EYES CLOSED

FACILITATOR DIALOGUE:

"Find a new partner. This is a continuation of the Trust Walk in Exercise Four. However, this time the follower must close his/her eyes. Leaders, you have a special responsibility to keep your partners safe and comfortable. Be aware of your partner and the direction in which you are leading them. Remember the FREEZE word."

FACILITATOR NOTE: Be sure to look out for the safety of the group. Play more music for them while they work on this exercise. Check with the group. If they want to go longer than just one song have them change partners.

PROCESSING QUESTIONS:

1. How comfortable were you closing your eyes?
2. Did you keep them closed?
3. How did you know you could trust this person?
4. What advice might you give them to help them be a better leader?
5. How would you have felt if we had started the workshop with this movement exercise?
6. Could you have done it?
7. What did you need in order to trust your partner?
8. What would enable people to trust you more?

EXERCISE SIX: CONTACT

FACILITATOR DIALOGUE:

"This last session is one of the most advanced. It is a complete expression of trust and teamwork on the part of the entire group. Not all groups get to where you are and not all groups are willing to go to this level. Congratulations!"

DEMONSTRATION: Ask for three volunteers. Choose one for your partner, and pair the other two. Choose two leaders and two followers. Begin by having the leaders guide their followers around the room using touch. Followers should keep their eyes closed. Leaders should watch out for the safety of their partners. (Remember the FREEZE word.) When one leader makes eye contact with another leader in the group, it is a silent agreement to trade partners without letting their partner know that they are being traded (as best as possible).

FACILITATOR NOTE: When two leaders acknowledge through eye contact that they are going to switch partners, they should move toward one another and determine how the switch will be made. The follower must always have some point of contact with one of the leaders. This will take some practice. Slow music is best here until they get the hang of this exercise.

FACILITATOR DIALOGUE:

"Choose a new partner and decide who will lead and who will follow. If you are being led, it's important to relax and not be too stiff. As a follower, try to keep your eyes closed to allow the process to happen. Leaders, be careful when you make eye contact. It's considered a contract, and you can't change your mind in the middle of the flow. You must clearly communicate your willingness or unwillingness to switch partners. If you don't want to change leaders, you can do this by looking away or down or shaking your head no."

PROCESSING QUESTIONS:

1. Leaders, how did that feel? Followers, how did that feel?
2. Were you concerned or scared?
3. How do you feel about the rest of the group now?
4. How do you feel about your ability to work together?

5. Do you have a better understanding for one another?
6. What have you learned about yourself?
7. What have you learned about others in your team?
8. Can you guess who led you around and how many times you were switched?

FACILITATOR NOTE: Have the participants change the leader role. Watch the group carefully to be sure everyone understands what to do. Start the music.

PROCESSING QUESTIONS:
1. How was it for you former followers to lead the former leaders?
2. Did you feel like you wanted to get them back or show them how it was done?
3. Those that were followers during this exercise, how was it for you having been in the lead position first? Were you more relaxed? More reluctant? Worried or scared?
4. What did you learn about yourself this time around?

FACILITATOR NOTE: Take a break. Refreshments. Come back to the circle to share.

FINAL DEBRIEFING

Invite the group to sit in a circle and share their experiences.

1. Does anyone want to share anything about this experience?
2. Did you ever think you'd do something like this?
3. Did you like it?
4. How do you feel this will help you as a team?
5. How are you changed by virtue of this experience?
6. What are some pros?
7. What are some cons?
8. How comfortable are you with your role as a leader?
9. How comfortable are you with your role as a follower?
10. Some leaders were creative in their leadership and brought out a great deal of play and creativity in their followers. Others were much more careful and intentional. Some styles work well for some, where others don't. Did you find your style?
11. What does a leader require from a follower?
12. What do followers require from leaders?
13. How was leading and following a collaborative effort here today?

FACILITATOR NOTE: As a facilitator, it's important to bring out in each session the questions that direct the best experience for the group. Each session will bring out certain truths that are important to acknowledge. It is vital that the participants, as part of a self-discovery process, give the answers the facilitator is looking for.

LOOK FOR THESE BENEFITS TO DRAW OUT OF THE EXPERIENCE:

1. Building rapport, collaborative leadership opportunities.
2. Building morale among workers, after downsizing or mergers.
3. Respecting diversity, finding common ground among people who are collaborating to accomplish a task or project.
4. Creating feelings of equality and respect among different levels of company employees—supervisors and staff.
5. Relieving tensions around gender issues or harassment issues in the work place.
6. Giving new supervisors a chance to test their wings in a nonthreatening way.
7. Pointing out that confidence, trust, vulnerability, observations rather than judgment and risk-taking all go along with building skills. A new skill cannot be built without these qualities present.

SOME PITFALLS TO WATCH FOR:

1. Participants that have never had an experiential training opportunity.
2. Participants that don't feel like they can dance. This is why we don't use the "D" word.

3. Participants of various age groups that have health concerns and sometimes there can be a generation gap issue to deal with.

EVALUATION:
As a matter of good teaching, the facilitator will want the participants to evaluate the benefits of the training s/he has just experienced. Some suggested categories for evaluation are:

1. Communication
2. Trust
3. Team building
4. Listening skills
5. Development of nonverbal skills
6. Building self-esteem
7. Breaking down barriers
8. Identifying management styles

CLOSING:
Leading participants through this experience can be a blessing in many ways. We have literally lead hundreds of people through this series of exercises. We can think of many comments and compliments that participants have given after going through this experience, but one that sticks out above the rest was a man who happened to work in a local industrial plant. He had never done anything like this before and was reluctant at best. Afterwards, he expressed his appreciation because his wife had a rare disease that was causing her to lose her sight. He expressed that this experience was the first he had to really begin to understand what she was going through, and he found himself being more compassionate and understanding toward her experience. He was very grateful. Sometimes the most important thing we need to do is get up out of our chairs, from behind our desks, and MOVE!

ACKNOWLEDGMENT: Steve Paxton and Nancy Stark Smith, the grandfather and grandmother of Contact Improvisation.

About the Creators of Contact:

HARLAN BROWNLEE is the Artistic Director of Programming for the Kansas City Chapter of Young Audiences. His responsibilities include developing and evaluating programs and workshops for students as well as professional development for both teachers and artists. He conducts professional development workshops for teachers on the infusion of dance in curriculum and has been recognized for his excellence in teaching and leading professional development workshops for the Kennedy Center in Washington, D.C. Currently, Harlan is pursuing his Master's degree in Education Research at the University of Missouri-Kansas City.

KELLY ELLISON has been the Outreach Specialist for the Children's Peace Pavilion since 1999. She brings a wealth of expertise to the program in the areas of curriculum development and service learning. Her primary responsibility is the Pledge School program, a program she created to serve local elementary schools with peace-related curriculum. Kelly is an experienced trainer and facilitator and has served as Executive Director and consultant for several nonprofit youth education programs. Kelly is currently an Executive Fellow completing her MBA at Rockhurst University, Kansas City, MO.

APPENDIXES
REFERENCES
INDEX

LEGEND

- [person icon] SMALL GROUP
- [person icon] MEDIUM GROUP
- [person icon] LARGE GROUP
- [person icon] ANY SIZE GROUP
- [S box] SMALL SPACE
- [M box] MEDIUM SPACE
- [L box] LARGE SPACE
- [GSD box] GROUP SIZE DEPENDENT

NAME OF ACTIVITY	SPIRITUAL FOCUS	SPACE REQUIRED	GROUP SIZE
20 THINGS I LOVE TO DO	balance	[Any Size]	[GSD]
BODY PARTS	gifts/service	[Any Size]	[GSD]
BOUNDARIES	beliefs/boundaries	[Any Size]	[GSD]
CAUSE & EFFECT	choice/accountability	[Any Size]	[GSD]
CLIQUES	appreciating diversity	[Large] [Large]	[M] [L]
COMPANIONS ON THE JOURNEY	blessing for the journey/faith	[Large]	[S] [L]
CONGA LINE	mentoring/guidance	[Any Size]	[S]
COOPERATIVE DRAWING	letting go/open mindedness	[Large]	[GSD]
COOPERATIVE PUZZLES	community/compassion	[Small] [Large]	[GSD]
DEPENDING ON YOU	the circle/sacred symbol	[Small] [Large]	[S] [M]
FACE TO FACE/BACK TO BACK	acceptance/empathy	[Large]	[M]
HERDING KITTENS	prayer/meditation	[Any Size]	[GSD]

LEGEND

- Small Group
- Medium Group
- Large Group
- Any Size Group
- S = Small Space
- M = Medium Space
- L = Large Space
- GSD = Group Size Dependent

NAME OF ACTIVITY	SPIRITUAL FOCUS	SPACE REQUIRED	GROUP SIZE
HOLY MACKEREL	seeking truth/spiritual growth	Small Group / Medium Group	M, L
IF EVER...	reconciliation/forgiveness	Any Size	GSD
INNER COMPASS	inner compass/living in the moment	Small Group / Medium Group	M, L
NUMBERMANIA	seeing God in all things	Any Size	GSD
ORB-IT	surrender/selflessness	Small Group / Medium Group	M, L
PASSAGES	trusting/listening	Small Group / Medium Group	L
PEACEABLE WORLD	peace	Small Group / Medium Group	M, L
SANTICKY, FANTICKY, LIM PO PO	following	Small Group / Medium Group	M, L
SHOE HOLLER	discernment/focus	Small Group / Medium Group	L
STEPPING STONES	stepping out in faith	Small Group / Medium Group	L
TIN PAN, BANG, BANG	compassion/inclusion	Any Size	GSD
TURNING OVER A NEW LEAF	change/transition	Small Group / Medium Group	M, L
YOU ARE ON THE OTHER SIDE	prayer	Small Group / Medium Group	M, L

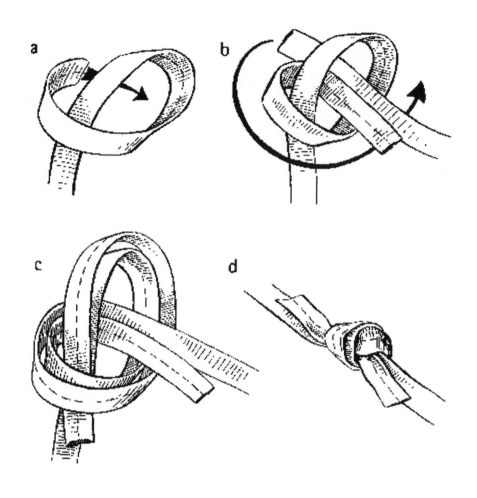

Diagram for tying a water knot.

APPENDIX B, RACCOON CIRCLES

You will find that several activities refer to **webbing circles** or **Raccoon Circles**. Many cultures of the world consider the circle to be a sacred symbol. In North American culture the circle is experienced in many ways, from "Ring around the Rosy" as a kindergartner to singing Kum Ba Yah circled up around a camp fire. We continue to gather in circles, play in circles and find new and exciting ways to create unity and fun in circles.

One of the more recent expressions of circles in our culture can be found in a set of games and initiatives called "Raccoon Circles." Raccoon Circles are formed by tying the ends of a 12 to 15 foot piece of tubular climbing webbing together to form a circle. Like any good initiative, if you look back you can find someone who has taken an idea and given it a forum that is usable and powerful. Tom Smith has done this for Raccoon Circles. Jim Cain has expanded and elaborated on his work. Both of these individuals have contributed in rich ways to the experiential education field and have numerous resources that go much deeper and farther in using Raccoon Circles.

 You will find that the various activities implementing the Raccoon Circle issue a warning about the importance of safety. How you tie the ends of the webbing together is an integral component of this safety. The knot required for safe use of the webbing circle is referred to as a water knot. See the diagram on the opposite page for the appropriate technique.

REFERENCES

Ash, Mel. *Shaving the Inside of Your Skull.* New York, NY: G.P. Putnam's Sons, 1996.

Beaver, R. Pierce, ed. *Eerdmans' Handbook to The World Religions.* Grand Rapids, MI: William B. Eerdmans Publishing Company, 1994.

Beers, V. Gilbert. *Touch Point Bible: A quick reference Bible.* Wheaton, IL: Tyndale House Publishers, Inc., 1996.

Bergman, John, and Saul Hewish. *Challenging Experience: An experiential approach to the treatment of serious offenders.* Oklahoma City, OK: Wood 'N' Barnes Publishing & Distribution, 2003.

Biedermann, Hans. *Dictionary of Symbolism: Cultural icons and the meanings behind them.* New York, NY: Meridian, 1994.

Bowker, John, ed.. *The Oxford Dictionary of World Religions.* New York, NY: Oxford University Press, 1999.

Brussat, Frederic and Mary Ann Brussat. *Spiritual Literacy: Reading the sacred in everyday life.* New York, NY: Touchstone, 1996.

Cain, Jim, and Tom Smith. *The Book on Raccoon Circles.* Tulsa, OK: Learning Unlimited, 2002.

Cavert, Chris. *Games (& other stuff) for Group, Book 2.* Oklahoma City, OK: Wood 'N' Barnes Publishing & Distribution, 1998.

Cavert, Chris. *Games (& other stuff) for Group, Book 1, Revised.* Oklahoma City, OK: Wood 'N' Barnes Publishing & Distribution, 1999.

Cavert, Chris. *Affordable Portables: A working book of initiative activities and problem solving elements, Revised.* Oklahoma City, OK: Wood 'N' Barnes Publishing & Distribution, 1999.

Cavert, Chris, and Laurie Frank. *Games (& other stuff) for Teachers: Classroom activities that promote pro-social learning.* Oklahoma City, OK: Wood 'N' Barnes Publishing & Distribution, 1999.

Cousineau, Phil, ed. *The Soul of the World: A modern book of hours.* New York, NY: Harper Collins Publishers, 1993.

Crompton, Samuel Willard. *100 Spiritual Leaders Who Shaped World History.* San Mateo, CA: Bluewood Books, 2001.

Cummings, e.e.. *100 Selected Poems.* New York, NY: Grove Press, 1954.

Frank, Laurie S. *The Caring Classroom: Using adventure to create community in the classroom.* Beverly, MA: GOAL Consulting, Project Adventure, Inc., 2001.

Freke, Timothy. *Spiritual Traditions: Essential teachings to transform your life.* New York, NY: Sterling Publishing Company, Inc., 2000.

Gerstein, Jackie. *A Place of Connection: Expressive counseling techniques for families and individuals.* Oklahoma City, OK: Wood 'N' Barnes Publishing & Distribution, 1998.

Grimbol, William R. *The Complete Idiot's Guide to Spirituality for Teens.* Indianapolis, IN: Alpha Books, 2000.

Hanh, Thich Nhat. *Peace is Every Step: The path of mindfulness in everyday life.* New York, NY: Bantam Books, 1992.

Huang, Chungliang Al, and Jerry Lynch. *Mentoring: The TAO of giving and receiving wisdom.* New York, NY: HarperSanFrancisco, 1995

Kidd, Sue Monk. *When the Heart Waits.* New York, NY: HarperSanFrancisco, 1990.

Langley, Myrtle. *Eyewitness Books: Religion.* New York, NY: Alfred A. Knopf, Inc., 1996.

Lonegren, Sig. *Labyrinth: Ancient myths and modern uses, Rev. Ed.* New York, NY: Sterling Publishing Company, Inc., 2001.

McFarlane, Marilyn. *Sacred Myths: Stories of World Religions.* Portland, OR: Sibyl Publications, Inc., 1996.

Miner, Todd, and Simon Priest. *Experiential Quotes: Words of wisom to live and work by.* Lakebay, WA: eXperientia Publications, 2000.

Peter, Val J., and Tom Dowd. *Boundaries: A guide for teens.* Boys Town, NE: The Boys Town Press, 2000.

Peterson, Eugene H. *The Message: The New Testament in contemporary language.* Colorado Spring, CO: NavPress, 1993.

Reath, Mary. *Public Lives Private Prayers.* Notre Dame, IN: Sorin Books, 2001.

Rohnke, Karl. *Funn Stuff. Vol. 2.* Dubuque, Iowa: Kendall/Hunt Publishing Company, 1996.

Rohnke, Karl, and Steve Butler. *Quicksilver: Adventure games, initiative problems, trust activities and a guide to effective leadership.* Dubuque, Iowa: Kendall/Hunt Publishing Company, 1995.

Sands, Helen Raphael. *The Healing Labyrinth: Finding your path to inner peace.* Hauppauge, NY: Barrons Educational Inc., 2001.

Schaper, Donna. *Labyrinths from the Outside In: Walking to spiritual insight, a beginner's guide.* Woodstock, VT: Skyligh Paths Publishers, 2000.

Schoel, Jim, Dick Prouty, and Paul Radcliffe. *Islands of Healing: A guide to adventure based counseling.* Hamilton, MA: Project Adventure, Inc., 1988.

Shaw, Maura D. *Ten Amazing People and How They Changed the World.* Woodstock, VT: SkyLight Paths Publishing, 2002.

Smith, Robert Lawrence. *A Quaker Book of Wisdom: Life lessons in simplicity, service, and common sense.* New York, NY: Eagle Brook, 1998

Telesco, Patricia. *Labyrinth Walking: Patterns of power.* Secaucus, NY: Citadel Press, 2001.

Templeton, John Marks, ed. *Worldwide Worship.* Radnor, PA: Templeton Foundation Press, 2000.

Theophane the Monk. *Tales of a Magic Monastery.* New York, NY: The Crossroad Publishing Company, 1981.

Toropov, Brandon, and Father Luke Buckles. *The Complete Idiot's Guide to World Religions.* 2d ed. Indianapolis, IN: Alpha Books, 2002.

Vardey, Lucinda, ed. *God in all Worlds: An anthology of contemporary spiritual writing.* New York, NY: Vintage Books, 1995.

Wehreheim, Carol A. *Getting It Together.* Louisville, KY: Westminster John Know Press, 2002.

Welch, Reuben. *We Really Do Need Each Other.* Grand Rapids, MA: Zondervan Publishing House, 1973.

Wilkinson, Philip. *Illustrated Dictionary of Religions.* New York, NY: DK Publishing, Inc., 1990.

Woods, Ralph L., ed. *The World Treasury of Religious Quotations.* New York City, NY: Hawthorn Books, Inc., 1966.

TIM DODDS and **LISA PROSSER-DODDS** have been working with children and youth for over twenty years. As professional educators, Tim worked for years in an at-risk education program in an inner city middle school. Lisa has been a school counselor in urban and suburban settings since 1994. Both are ordained ministers and have been active in youth ministry together since 1982. They have worked with groups of children and youth in faith-based settings around the world. Tim is known in the camping field for his work in staff training and development. He is a sought after trainer and program development specialist. Lisa brings over ten years of experience as a Licensed Professional Counselor working with children, youth and families in her private practice. She also served as the director of the Children's Peace Pavilion, traveling worldwide teaching the concepts of peaceable parenting. She, too, is a sought after speaker and trainer in the education, ministry and counseling fields.

In 2001, Tim and Lisa formed *Journeys Personal Counseling and Consulting, L.L.C.* Journeys provides direct counseling services to those interested in personal growth or who are in the midst of life transitions. They also provide consulting and training for educators, clergy, camping professionals and others who work with children, youth and families.